Egyptian Hieroglyphs

1 Limestone wall panel, decorated with figures and hieroglyphs, from the tomb of a man called Iry. Fifth Dynasty. H. 95 cm. BM 1168.

Egyptian Hieroglyphs

W. V. Davies

University of California Press/British Museum

Preface

The limitations of this book should be stated at the outset. It is simply too brief to do justice to a system of communication as complex and many-sided as the hieroglyphic writing of ancient Egypt. The account of the subject presented here has had to be very selective, covering, in an introductory manner, only those areas that I believe to be of the greatest importance and interest. For more detailed and scholarly treatments of the various aspects of the system, readers are recommended to consult the works listed in the Bibliography.

In the preparation of the book I have been kindly and ably assisted in various ways by a number of colleagues. Mr T. G. H. James made several valuable suggestions concerning its organization and content; Professor A. F. Shore and Miss Carol Andrews provided information on Coptic and demotic matters; Mrs Christine Barratt drew the line illustrations and the hieroglyphs in the text; Mr Peter Hayman prepared the bulk of the photographic material; Miss Felicity Jay typed the final copy; members of the staff of British Museum Publications skilfully expedited the book's completion and its progress through the press. To all these I offer grateful thanks, as I do also to those institutions who have allowed me to use illustrations of objects in their collections.

i'm Rhieni â diolch

University of California Press
Berkeley and Los Angeles California

© 1987 The Trustees of the British Museum

Third impression 1989

Designed by Arthur Lockwood
Front cover design by Grahame Dudley

Printed in Great Britain

Library of Congress Cataloguing-in-Publication Data
Davies, W. V.
  Egyptian hieroglyphs.
  (Reading the past; v. 6)
  Bibliography: p.
  Includes index.
  1. Egyptian language—Writing, Hieroglyphic
2. Egyptian language—Writing. I. Title. II. Series.
PJ1097.D4   1987   493'.1   87-24352
  ISBN 0-520-06287-6

Contents

1
The Language

Ancient Egyptian occupies a special position among the languages of the world. It is not only one of the very oldest recorded languages (probably only Sumerian is older) but it also has a documented history longer by far than that of any other. It was first written down towards the end of the fourth millennium BC and thereafter remained in continuous recorded use down to about the eleventh century AD, a period of over 4,000 years. Egyptian, or Coptic (as the last stage of the language is called), expired as a spoken tongue during the Middle Ages, when it was superseded by Arabic. It is now, strictly, a dead language, though it continues to 'live on', albeit in a fossilised form, in the liturgy of the Coptic church in Egypt. Although it can only be a minute fraction of what was actually produced, the body of written material to have survived in Egyptian is, nevertheless, enormous. It consists, in large part, of religious and funerary texts, but it also includes secular documents of many different types – administrative, business, legal, literary and scientific – as well as private and official biographical and historical inscriptions. This record is our most important single source of evidence on ancient Egyptian society.

Since the decipherment of the writing system in the third decade of the last century (see Chapter 5), the language has been among the most thoroughly researched areas of Egyptology. As a result, although a great deal of vocabulary and many points of grammar remain to be fully elucidated, our understanding of the basic structure of Egyptian and of the rules governing its operation can now be considered to be on a reasonably firm footing. It is not only Egyptologists who have taken an interest in the language. In recent years increasing attention has been paid to Egyptian by linguists concerned with the study of human language as a general phenomenon. In this area, Egyptian is of particular importance to comparative and historical linguists, its longevity offering a rare opportunity for the testing of theories concerning the nature and rate of language change and development.

Egyptian is one of a group of African and Near Eastern languages (many of them still living tongues) which have sufficient similarities in their grammar and vocabulary to suggest that they are derived from a common linguistic ancestor. This group is known to scholars as Afro-Asiatic (or Hamito-Semitic). The Afro-Asiatic family is deemed at present to consist of six co-ordinate branches, of which Ancient Egyptian forms one. The other five are: Semitic (sub-branches of which include such well-known languages as Akkadian, Hebrew and Arabic), Berber (found in north Africa to the west of Egypt), Chadic (found in the sub-Saharan regions to the east, south and west of Lake Chad), Cushitic (found in the Sudan, Ethiopia, Somalia and north-west Kenya) and Omotic (found in southern Ethiopia). Of these, only Egyptian and Semitic are favoured with substantial written traditions; in the case of the others, written sources are minimal or even non-existent and a great deal of basic recording and analysis still remains to be achieved. There is as yet no consensus as to the date when the various branches separated from the proto-language. Recent estimates, based largely on the degree of differentiation between early Egyptian and Akkadian (the oldest recorded form of Semitic), vary widely. One scholar has placed the likely date of separation at around 6000 BC, another at around 12000 BC.

There is no evidence that the ancient Egyptians took a serious interest in the analysis of their own language. If works of grammar, such as those written in antiquity for Greek

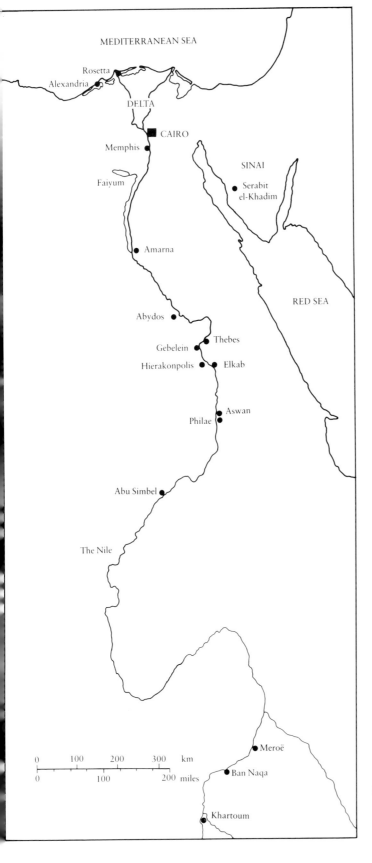

2 Egypt and the Sudan.

8

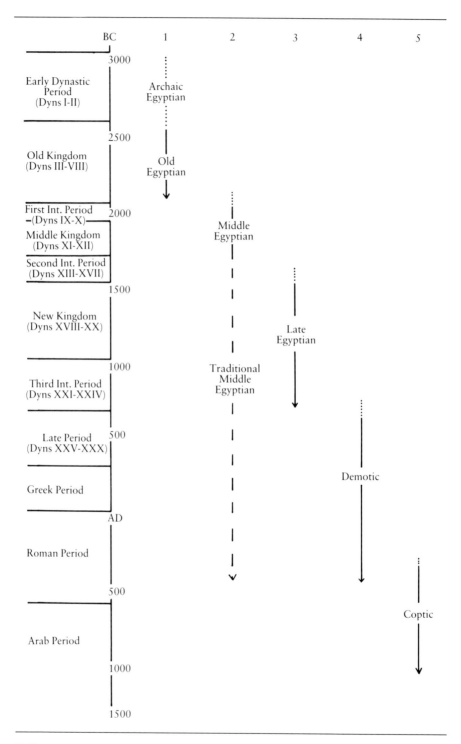

Table 1: Stages in the development of the Egyptian language.

and Latin, were composed for Egyptian, they have not survived. Our knowledge of Ancient Egyptian is entirely the product of modern scholarship. Egyptologists identify five, somewhat arbitrary, stages in the development of the language (see table opposite), each characterised by certain distinctive features of grammar and orthography, with the most fundamental point of division perceived as lying between the first two stages, on the one hand, and the last three, on the other. They have been arrived at by analysis and comparison of a large number of dated texts, covering the whole period of the recorded use of the language. Scholars, engaged in such work, have had always to keep in mind that the evidence at every stage consists of the language as *written*, and that written language rarely corresponds exactly to the spoken variety. Written language is more conservative: it frequently includes spellings that are partly or even wholly historical as well as words and grammatical constructions that have long ceased to be used in actual speech. Such redundancy is well evidenced in the case of Egyptian. In the following outline of the five stages it should be noted that the language of the very earliest inscriptions (from the late Predynastic and Early Dynastic Periods (*c.* 3100–2650 BC)), sometimes called 'Archaic Egyptian', is not included as a stage. This is because the inscriptions in question are too brief and limited in content to allow any meaningful analysis of the underlying language.

Old Egyptian
The language of the inscriptions of the Old Kingdom (*c.* 2650–2135 BC), the period in which the first continuous texts appear.

Middle Egyptian
The idiom, in particular, of the First Intermediate Period and the Middle Kingdom (*c.* 2135–1785 BC); regarded as the 'classical' stage of the language, used in literary, religious and monumental inscriptions through to the Graeco-Roman Period. Very close to Old Egyptian in structure.

Late Egyptian
The everyday language of the New Kingdom and Third Intermediate Period (*c.* 1550–700 BC), as witnessed particularly in secular documents of the Ramesside Period (*c.* 1300–1080 BC); also found to some extent in literary and monumental inscriptions. Very different from Old and Middle Egyptian, especially in its verbal structure.

Demotic
Vernacular successor of Late Egyptian, written in the script known as Demotic (see below, Chapter 2), attested from the beginning of the Late Period down to late Roman times (*c.* 700 BC—fifth century AD).

Coptic
The final stage of the language, as written in the Coptic script (see below, Chapter 2), from the third century AD onwards. The only stage of the language of which the vocalic structure is known and in which distinct dialects are recognisable. The two major dialects are: Sahidic, the standard literary dialect until the tenth century AD, its place of origin uncertain, possibly Thebes or Memphis; and Bohairic, originally the dialect of the west Delta, which supplanted Sahidic as the official dialect in the eleventh century.

2
The Scripts

By the Late Period of Egyptian history three distinct scripts were in use for writing the Egyptian language. They are known as hieroglyphic, hieratic and demotic respectively. They are superficially different from each other in appearance but actually represent the same writing system, hieratic and demotic being merely cursive derivatives of hieroglyphic. All three were eclipsed during the Roman Period by a fourth script, called Coptic, which was based on the Greek alphabet and operated on quite different principles. The present chapter will be devoted mainly to an account of some of the more important external features and conventions of the scripts; the principles underlying the native system will be dealt with in the next chapter.

Hieroglyphic

This was the earliest form of Egyptian script, and it was also the longest-lived. The first hieroglyphs appear in the late Predynastic Period, in the form of short label-texts on stone and pottery objects from various sites, probably to be dated within the range 3100–3000 BC, while the last datable examples are to be found in a temple inscription on the island of Philae carved in AD 394, nearly three and a half thousand years later. Originally the script was employed to write different kinds of texts, in a variety of media, but as its cursive version, hieratic, developed, hieroglyphic was increasingly confined to religious and monumental contexts, where it was rendered most typically in carved relief in stone. It was for this reason that the ancient Greeks called the individual elements of the script *ta hiera grammata*, 'the sacred letters', or *ta hieroglyphica*, 'the sacred carved (letters)', from which our terms 'hieroglyph' and 'hieroglyphic' are derived.

The signs of the hieroglyphic script are largely pictorial or 'iconic' in character. A few are of indeterminate form and origin, but most are recognisable pictures of natural or man-made objects, which, when carefully executed, may exhibit fine detail and colouring, although they are conventionalised in form and their colour is not always realistic. There is little doubt that the best examples of the script have 'an intrinsic beauty of line and colour' that fully justifies the claim, often made, that 'Egyptian hieroglyphic writing is the most beautiful ever designed'. Its pictorial character should not, however, mislead one into thinking that the script is a kind of primitive 'picture-writing'. It is a full writing system, capable of communicating the same kinds of complex linguistic information as our own alphabet, though it does so by different means. Typologically the script is a 'mixed' system, which means that its constituents do not all perform the same function; some of the signs convey meaning, others convey sound (see Chapter 3).

The system was never limited to a fixed number of hieroglyphs. It contained a relatively stable core of standard signs throughout its history, but, in addition, new signs were invented as required, while others fell into disuse. Developments in material culture were influential in this process. Innovations in Egyptian weaponry at the beginning of the New Kingdom, for example, saw the introduction of hieroglyphs for the horse and chariot, 🐎, and for a new type of sword, ⛏. By the same process, other hieroglyphs became obsolete and were either changed in form or entirely replaced; the sign for the royal *khepresh*-crown was ⛑ in the Thirteenth Dynasty and ⛑ in the

Eighteenth Dynasty; the sign for the common razor was ⊂⊃ in the Old Kingdom, ⊂⊃ in the Middle Kingdom, and finally ⊓ in the New Kingdom. In these cases developments in fashion and technology produced corresponding changes in the script, each sign in turn depicting the current form of the actual object. There was no consistency in the process, however. Many hieroglyphs, even those in culture-sensitive categories, retained a more or less regular form; others changed temporarily and then reverted. The common hieroglyph depicting scribal equipment, for example, was written ⬚ in the Old Kingdom, 'up-dated' to ⬚ in the First Intermediate Period, and then changed back to the Old Kingdom form, which remained standard thereafter.

Taken over the whole period of the script's use, the total number of known hieroglyphs is huge; over 6,000 have so far been documented. The figure is misleading, however. The vast majority of these signs are found only on the temple walls of the Graeco-Roman Period, when, perhaps for special religious and esoteric reasons, the number of hieroglyphs was deliberately increased. In earlier periods the repertoire in standard use at any one time was always fewer than 1,000 (for example, about 700 are attested for the period covered by Middle Egyptian proper), and of these only a relatively small proportion occurs with real frequency.

3 *Left* Temple inscription carved in AD 394. These are the latest firmly dated hieroglyphs yet attested. They label a representation of a god, whom they name as 'Merul, son of Horus'. Temple of Philae.

4 *Right* Inscription in a tomb of the early New Kingdom including some of the very earliest examples of hieroglyphs representing the chariot and the horse. Elkab.

A hieroglyphic inscription is arranged either in columns or in horizontal lines, the former being the more ancient arrangement. The sequence of signs is continuous. There are no punctuation marks or spaces to indicate the divisions between words. Orientation is usually rightward, with the individual signs and the inscription of which they form a part read from right to left, and with upper taking precedence over lower. It has been suggested by one authority that this preference for rightward orientation is derived from the fact that human beings are generally right-handed; quite simply, in producing a text, 'the scribe began on the side where the hand that did the writing happened to be situated'. Leftward orientation does also occur but as a rule only in certain contexts; it was employed, for example, in inscriptions that accompany figures facing left, or to provide balance or symmetry in a larger composition. Examples of horizontal and columnar inscriptions orientated in both directions are given below. The direction of writing is indicated as well as the order in which the signs are to be read. It will be seen

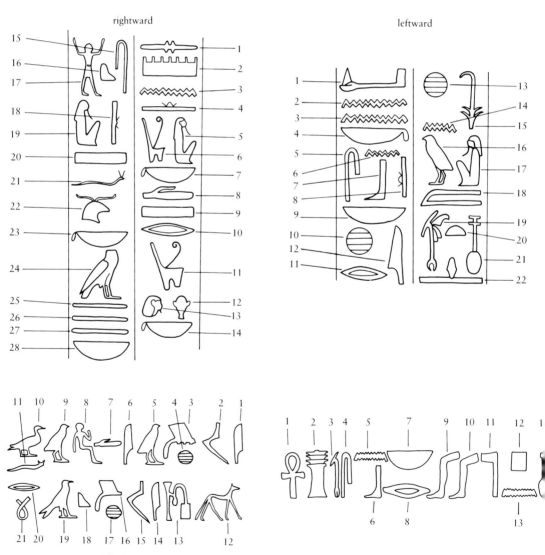

5 Examples of columnar and horizontal inscriptions, in rightward and leftward orientation. The numbers indicate the order in which the signs are to be read.

that a clue to the direction of reading is given by those signs, especially human or animal, that have a recognisable front and rear. Such signs in normal writing always face the beginning of the inscription.

Aesthetic or calligraphic considerations played a large part in the internal organisation of an inscription. Hieroglyphs were not written in linear sequence, one after another, like the letters of an alphabetic script, but were grouped into imaginary squares or rectangles so as to ensure the most harmonious arrangement and to minimise the possibility of unsightly gaps. Such requirements affected the relative size and proportions of individual signs and determined whether a word was written in full or in an abbreviated form. It is not uncommon to find hieroglyphs switched in their order for reasons of better spacing. Indeed 'graphic transposition', as it is called, is virtually the rule for some sign combinations, particularly those in which a bird hieroglyph is written next to a small squat sign or a tall thin one. Many such transpositions were initially designed to make the most effective use of space in columnar inscriptions, but became so standard that they were often retained in horizontal texts as well.

Sign order was similarly affected by considerations of prestige. Words for entities of high status (such as 'king', 'god', and the names of specific gods) were usually given precedence in writing over words which, in speech, they followed. Typical examples

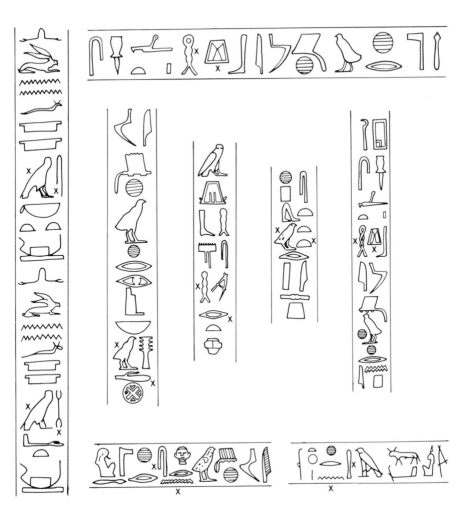

6 Examples of graphic transposition. The transposed signs are marked with a cross.

occur in the lines of an inscription on a tomb panel belonging to a man called Iry (written

1, 7 [hieroglyphs]). The first three signs of the inscription form the beginning of a common funerary formula which translates as 'An offering which Anubis gives'. In the order of signs the jackal hieroglyph occupies initial position in the group, whereas the word it represents, 'Anubis', actually comes third in the order of Egyptian speech. The jackal takes precedence because Anubis is a god. Similarly in the group [hieroglyphs], which is a title meaning 'priest of the king', the hieroglyphs for 'king', [hieroglyphs], are written before the hieroglyph for 'priest', [hieroglyphs], in reversal again of the actual word order. Graphic reversals of this kind are referred to as 'honorific transposition'.

The hieroglyphic script was always more than just a writing system. The Egyptians referred to it as [hieroglyphs], 'writing of the divine words', or simply as [hieroglyphs], 'divine words'. The individual hieroglyph was termed [hieroglyphs], 'sign', 'image', 'form', the same word as was sometimes used to denote a representation in Egyptian art. This terminology reflects two points of fundamental importance about the script: it was closely related to representational art and, like the art, it was endowed with religious or magico-religious significance.

36 The interrelationship between art and writing, which can be seen already on some of the earliest inscribed monuments, is evident in a number of ways. Most obviously the hieroglyphs are themselves miniature pictures. In fact, in all essentials, they are small-scale versions of the larger 'actors' in an artistic scene. It is important to remember that Egyptian art was not a free form. It had a distinct purpose: to 'make to live' for eternity the things it depicted. In keeping with its purpose it was governed by strict rules as to content and manner of representation. A basic convention was that a figure should be depicted as objectively as possible, with no account taken of the effects of visual distortion. A figure was reproduced, two-dimensionally, in what was deemed to be its most 'characteristic' aspect; in the case of a complex figure, it might be necessary to embody more than one aspect in a single representation. The hieroglyphs follow this convention. Three instances, again from the inscriptions of Iry, may be taken to illustrate the point.

7 The sign below the jackal is a single hieroglyph with two parts. The lower rectangular part is a reed mat; the conical object centred above it is a loaf of bread. It is actually a picture of a loaf standing on a mat. The two are depicted, however, from different 'characteristic' view points. The loaf is shown in profile, the mat as if seen from above.

8 The same combination of views is apparent in the hieroglyph depicting items of scribal equipment. Side views are given of the narrow brush-holder and the round pigment bag, but a top view is shown of the rectangular palette with its characteristic paint-holes.

9 Even more illustrative is a third hieroglyph, representing an old man leaning on a stick. It is a very skilful carving, showing fine naturalistic detail, but it is not an organic whole. Close inspection will show that the figure is a composite, with the major parts of the body shown from different points of view. The head, the front breast, the arms and the legs are in profile view; the eye, the shoulders, and the rear breast in frontal; and the navel in three quarters. It is a picture of the body that combines in a single figure as many as possible of its essential aspects. The same diagrammatic approach informs the figures of Iry and his retinue on the same monument. It is the standard manner of representing the human body in Egyptian two-dimensional art.

The relationship between the figures and the hieroglyphs in the scene is not only a matter of internal structure. Each of the human figures has a separate inscription of its own, which identifies it by name and sometimes by title as well. The largest of the figures is identified as 'Priest of the king, Iry'. The smaller figure immediately in front of Iry is described as the 'scribe, Kai-nefer', the one behind as 'Iry-nedjes'. The three others

7 Panel of Iry. Detail of horizontal inscriptions at the top.

8 Panel of Iry. Detail of hieroglyph
representing scribal equipment.
H. 6.6 cm.

9 Panel of Iry. Detail of hieroglyph
representing an old man. H. 9.2 cm.

10 Limestone statuette of Min-nefret; view showing inscription on the right side. Fourth Dynasty. H. 47 cm. BM 65430.

11 *Left* Limestone stela of Wennekhu and his son Penpakhenty, the names in each case followed by a 'name determinative' (). Nineteenth Dynasty. H. 35.3 cm. BM 1248.

12 *Above* Granite squatting figure of Sennefer. Such statues, because of their peculiar 'block' form, came to be regarded as suitable vehicles for long texts. Eighteenth Dynasty. H. 83.8 cm. BM 48.

shown facing the tomb owner are, from top to bottom, 'Nen-kai', 'Nefer-seshem-nesut' and 'Itjeh' respectively. In each case the writing follows in general the direction of the figure to which it belongs – rightward in the case of Iry, Iry-nedjes and Kai-nefer, left-ward in that of the others. This correlation leads to a further point of identity. When a name occurs in an Egyptian inscription it is normally followed by a hieroglyph in the form of a male or female figure, called by Egyptologists a 'name determinative'. Its function is quite simply to clarify whether the name is that of a man or woman. In this case every one of the names lacks a small-scale determinative. The reason for this is that the larger figures, because of their proximity to the names, themselves act as determina-tives. In other words, they function as large-scale hieroglyphs.

This kind of interdependence is not confined to two dimensions. The statue of the lady Min-nefret shows the same principle at work in three dimensions. The statue is inscribed with hieroglyphs on the right and left sides of the seat. On each side the hieroglyphs are orientated in accordance with the figure. On the natural right side, they face rightwards; on the natural left, leftwards. The inscription ends with the lady's title and name, ⌂⌂⌂⌂⌂, 'the confidante of the king, Min-nefret'. Again there is no determinative, in this case because the statue serves as the determinative; it is actually here a three-dimensional hieroglyph.

The panel of Iry and the statue of Min-nefret both date to the Old Kingdom. This is the period when the relationship between art and writing is most consistently in evi-dence. The relationship remained in existence throughout the whole of Egyptian history but, after the Old Kingdom, a partial 'disengagement' gradually took place. Certain rules, such as those concerning orientation, continued to be observed, but there was an increasing tendency for the inscription on a monument to be treated as an entity in its own right. The virtual unity of name and figure was still sometimes respected on monu-ments as late as the New Kingdom, but more often than not it was disregarded and name determinatives were appended even when a figure of the name's owner was depicted nearby. At the same time texts began to 'take over' the statues on which they were inscribed. Whereas in the Old Kingdom inscriptions were appropriately situated, on the seat or the pedestal of a statue, from the Middle Kingdom onwards they intrude, inorganically, on to the dress of the owner and eventually on to the body itself. The impression is, in the case of certain statues, that the figure has been viewed as primarily a vehicle for the text that it bears.

As an integral part of a system of recreative art the hieroglyphs were naturally believed to have the power to bring to life what they depicted or stated. A funerary formula invoking benefits from a god was enough in itself, if written in hieroglyphs, to ensure the reception of those benefits by the deceased owner, as long as the owner was named, as in the case of Iry. The name of a person, inscribed in hieroglyphs, was believed to embody that person's unique identity. If the representation of a person lacked a name, it lacked also the means to ensure his continued existence in the after-life. To destroy the name(s) of a person was to deprive him of his identity and render him non-existent. On several occasions in Egyptian history the cartouches (name rings) of a dead ruler were systematically mutilated or removed from monuments on the orders of a vengeful successor. Even the gods were not immune from such attack. When King Akhenaten sought, in the late Eighteenth Dynasty, to institute a new religion of the sun disk and abolish the old regime, he ordered, among other things, that the name of the existing chief of the gods, Amun, be removed from the monuments of the land, with effects that can still be seen on many surviving pieces. By similar means the monument of one person was often appropriated for the use of another. The essential act in such 'usurpation' was the change of name. The name of the original owner was removed; the name of the new

13 Detail of a basalt statue of a man holding
a shrine. The hieroglyphic inscriptions
include the cartouches of King Amasis
deliberately effaced. Twenty-sixth
Dynasty. H. of shrine 27 cm. BM 134.

14 Red granite statue of King Amenophis II of the
Eighteenth Dynasty with inscriptions added by kings of
the Nineteenth Dynasty. H. 2.6 m. BM 61.

one added; the monument might otherwise be left untouched. A statue of a king in the British Museum provides a good example. On grounds of style and iconography it can be identified as a portrait of Amenophis II of the Eighteenth Dynasty (*c.* 1400–1350 BC). The cartouches it bears, however, are those of Ramesses II and Merenptah of the Nineteenth Dynasty (*c.* 1290–1200 BC). The statue was usurped for these later kings simply by adding their names; no attempt was made to change the appearance of the piece to make it conform to the style of their time.

Belief in the magical efficacy of the 'divine words' found further expression in the attempts that were occasionally made to limit the power of certain hieroglyphs, especially those depicting humans, birds and animals. These were deemed to have considerable potential for harm when located in magically 'sensitive' areas, like the walls of a burial chamber or the sides of a sarcophagus. The fear was that they might assume an independent hostile life of their own and consume the food offerings intended for the deceased or even attack the dead body itself. Steps were therefore taken to neutralise the danger that they posed. Sometimes such hieroglyphs were simply suppressed and replaced by anodyne substitutes. On other occasions they were modified in some way to immobilise them. The bodies of human figures and the heads of insects and snakes were omitted, the bodies of birds truncated, the bodies of certain animals severed in two, and the tails of snakes abbreviated. Particularly dangerous creatures, such as the evil serpent, called Apophis, the great enemy of the sun-god Rē', were sometimes shown as constrained or 'killed' by knives or spears.

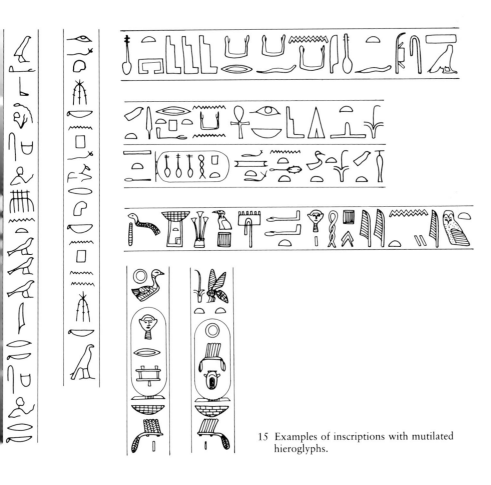

15 Examples of inscriptions with mutilated hieroglyphs.

Other hieroglyphs were regarded as having beneficial properties and were rendered in three dimensions to serve as amulets or charms. When worn on the body these amulets were believed to confer 'good luck' on their owners, whether living or dead. The amulet
16   in the form of the *sa*-sign, meaning 'protection', was one of several that offered protection against the powers of evil; the so-called *udjat*-eye of the god Horus was another.
17   The *ankh*- and the *djed*-signs offered the benefits of 'life' and 'endurance' respectively,
18, 19   while the hand, leg and face, and others like them, helped to restore the functions of the
19   bodily parts after death. The sign meaning 'horizon' shows the sun rising over a mountain. It allowed the deceased to witness and identify with the sun's daily rebirth and thereby be reborn himself.

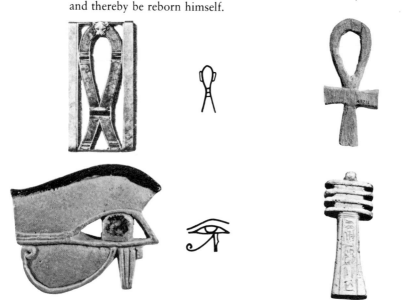

16–19 Amulets in the form of hieroglyphs.
16 *sa* (H. 3.9 cm, Cairo Museum, CG 52044, gold and semi-precious stones), *udjat* (H. 4.9 cm, BM 23092, faience).

17 *ankh* (H. 11 cm, BM 43211, wood), *djed* (H. 7.4 cm, BM 50742, faience).

18 hand H. 0.7 cm, BM 14703, carnelian), leg (H. 1.9 cm, BM 54747, carnelian).

19 face (H. 1.7 cm, BM 57812, steatite), horizon (H. 2 cm BM 8300, glass).

Hieratic

Hieratic is an adaptation of the hieroglyphic script, the signs being simplified to facilitate quick reproduction of a kind required in non-monumental contexts. It was Egypt's administrative and business script throughout most of its history, and was also employed to record documents of a literary, scientific and religious nature. It is found on all sorts of media, but most typically on rolls or sheets of papyrus or on bits of pottery and stone called ostraca. Documents in hieratic were usually written in black ink, applied by means of a brush made out of a stem of rush. Red ink was occasionally employed to mark out a special section, like the beginning of a text or a numerical total, or to indicate punctuation points in literary compositions. There are also monumental examples where the script was incised in stone, but these are quite rare and of a relatively late date.

20,21

The earliest substantial body of texts in hieratic yet attested are estate records of the Fourth Dynasty, although sporadic examples of the script are known from much earlier. Its origin clearly goes back to the very beginning of writing in Egypt, since the first stages in its development are observable in the semi-cursive hieroglyphs that occur as labels on vessels of the late Predynastic Period. The 'day-to-day' script of Egypt for nearly two and a half millennia, hieratic was finally ousted from secular use by another cursive script, demotic, at the beginning of the Late Period (*c.* 600 BC). Thereafter its use was confined to religious documents, which is why it was called *hieratika*, 'priestly', by the Greeks. The latest known hieratic documents are religious papyri dated to the third century AD. Like hieroglyphic, hieratic could be written either in columns or in horizontal lines but, unlike hieroglyphic, its orientation was invariable. Hieratic proper always reads from right to left. This is one of the features that distinguishes it from 'cursive hieroglyph', a script that resembles early hieratic and was the preferred form, for example, for reproducing certain kinds of funerary text (such as the Coffin Texts and the 'Book of the Dead') from the Middle Kingdom down to the Third Intermediate Period.

37

22

20 *Right* Scribe's palette of ivory. It has two holes, one for black ink, one for red, and a slot for holding brushes. On the bottom are scribal jottings in hieratic. Eighteenth Dynasty. H. 30 cm. BM 5524.

21 *Below* Scene from a tomb painting showing a scribe conducting a census of geese. He stands reading from an unrolled papyrus with his palette tucked under his arm. Thebes. Eighteenth Dynasty. H. of scribe's figure 33.4 cm. BM 37978.

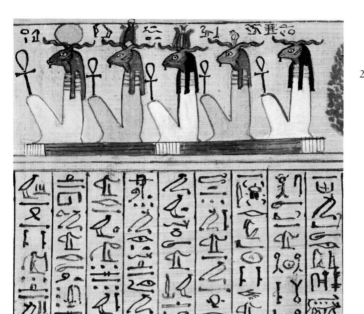

22 Cursive hieroglyphs in a 'Book of the Dead' of the Nineteenth Dynasty. The hieroglyphs accompanying the deities at the top are in leftward orientation. Those in the main text below are in rightward orientation. Papyrus of Hunefer. BM 9901,8.

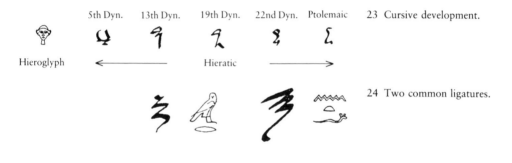

	5th Dyn.	13th Dyn.	19th Dyn.	22nd Dyn.	Ptolemaic

Hieroglyph ← Hieratic →

23 Cursive development.

24 Two common ligatures.

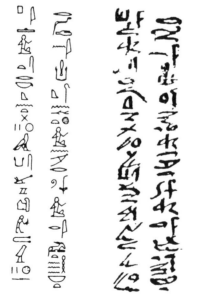

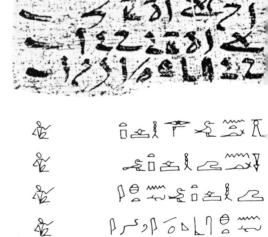

25 Section from a private letter in the hieratic script, written in columns on papyrus. Eleventh Dynasty. New York, Metropolitan Museum of Art.

26 Part of an inventory of names written in the hieratic script, in horizontal lines. Twelfth Dynasty. Papyrus Reisner I. Boston, Museum of Fine Arts.

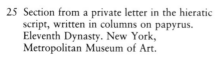

It is probably true to say that hieratic never completely lost touch with its monumental parent. It is always possible, with varying degrees of ease or difficulty, depending on the period and type of inscription, to transcribe a hieratic text sign by sign into its hieroglyphic equivalent. However, it followed its own course of evolution, the signs showing a definite tendency to become progressively more cursive, and it also developed other conventions and features appropriate to a running hand. Certain groups of two or more signs came to be rendered by one stroke of the brush in what are called 'ligatures', and complicated signs were often avoided or replaced by simple substitutes (for example, the bird was abbreviated to) – these in turn were sometimes borrowed by the hieroglyphic script, a reverse influence that is hardly surprising when it is considered that in all probability many hieroglyphic inscriptions were initially drafted in hieratic.

A crucial period in the history of hieratic was the Middle Kingdom. Up to the Eleventh Dynasty hieratic texts were usually written in columns. For some reason during the Twelfth Dynasty there was a major change in practice. Scribes began to write in horizontal lines, a mode that soon became universal. At the same time different styles of script began to appear, which developed along their own lines. By the New Kingdom they had become quite separate. One was a cursive 'business' hand used for writing mundane documents, the other an elegant 'book' hand employed for literary texts and in contexts where a 'traditional' hand was thought more appropriate. Out of the business hand of the late New Kingdom there developed in turn, during the Third Intermediate Period, two regional variants, both even more cursive – the so-called 'abnormal' hieratic in Upper Egypt and demotic in Lower Egypt. Abnormal hieratic was completely supplanted by demotic in the Twenty-sixth Dynasty, following the conquest of the south by kings of the north.

27 Line from a literary text. Nineteenth Dynasty. Papyrus d'Orbiney. BM 10183,3.

28 Papyrus with witness subscriptions in traditional hieratic (above) and abnormal hieratic (below). Twenty-sixth Dynasty. Papyrus Brooklyn 47.218.3. New York, The Brooklyn Museum.

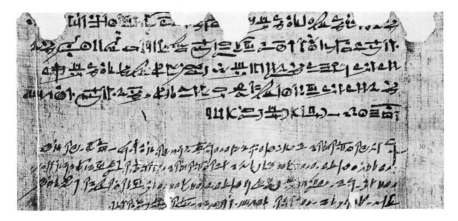

Demotic

For the rest of Egyptian history demotic was the only native script in general use for day-to-day purposes. The name demotic, ancient Greek *demotika*, 'popular (script)', refers to its secular functions, as does its Egyptian name *sḫ šʿt*, 'the writing of letters'. Like hieratic, demotic was mostly confined to use on papyri and ostraca and it maintained the scribal tradition of writing in horizontal lines with rightward orientation. It is otherwise an almost independent form, barely recognisable as a descendant of hieratic, let alone hieroglyphic. It is a very cursive script, almost wholly lacking in iconicity and replete with ligatures, abbreviations and other orthographic peculiarities, making it difficult to read and virtually impossible to transcribe meaningfully into any kind of hieroglyphic 'original'.

The demotic record is dominated by legal, administrative and commercial material. However, it also includes, from the Ptolemaic Period on, literary compositions, as well as scientific and even religious texts, which were written in a more calligraphic hand, the ink now increasingly applied with the reed pen introduced by the Greeks, which by the end of the period had virtually supplanted the traditional brush. Another development of the Ptolemaic Period was that the script began to be used monumentally, particularly on funerary and commemorative stelae. The best-known example is the so-called Rosetta Stone (see Chapter 5), which contains a single text, a priestly decree, repeated in three scripts, hieroglyphic, demotic and Greek (the latter included as Greek was now the official language of Egypt). All three versions, including the demotic, are incised in the stone. Present evidence suggests that demotic outlived the two other native scripts by a century or so before finally falling into disuse in the fifth century AD. The latest demotic inscription is a graffito in the temple of Philae dated to AD 450.

29 *Right* Demotic ostracon: a receipt for the delivery of wine in year ten of the Emperor Antoninus Pius. AD 145. H. 8.7 cm. BM 21426.

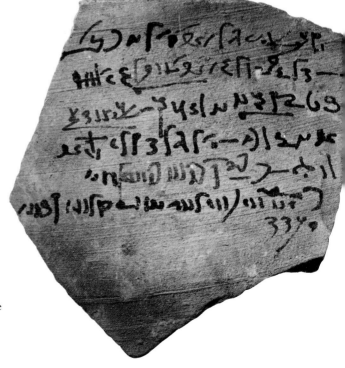

30 *Below* The reed pen introduced into Egypt by the Greeks. Traces of black ink survive on the tip of this example. Behnasa. 2nd century AD. L. 17.3 cm. BM 38145.

Coptic

As the old native scripts went into decline and finally disappeared during Egypt's Roman and Christian period, so a new script, Coptic, as used by the 'Copts', took their place to write the Egyptian language. The name 'Copt' is derived from the Arabic *gubti*, itself a corruption of the Greek *Aiguptios*. It means simply 'Egyptian'. It was the term used by the Arabs after their conquest of Egypt in the seventh century, to denote the native inhabitants of the country. Coptic represents a distinct departure from the other scripts. It consists of the twenty-four letters of the Greek alphabet, supplemented, in its standard, Sahidic, form, by six characters taken from demotic to denote Egyptian phonemes not known to Greek. It is thus a fully alphabetic script in which the vowels of the

31 Egyptian magical papyrus
written in Greek and demotic
letters. Behnasa. 2nd century
AD. H. 29 cm. BM 10808.

language are represented, as well as the consonants. The letters borrowed from demotic and their phonemic values are as follows:

Demotic	Coptic	Value
ʒ	ϣ	sh
ỿ	ϥ	f
?.	ϧ	h
ǀᴸ	ⳉ	j
ꝺ	ϭ	g
ⳤ	ϯ	ti

The development of this standard form of the alphabet, which was well established by the fourth century AD, is closely associated with the spread of Christianity in Egypt. It has been suggested that the impetus for its development was provided by the need to furnish translations of the New Testament and other religious texts for the native population in a regularised and easily accessible form, a task for which the demotic script appears to have been considered both inadequate and inappropriate. The Coptic script was not, however, initially devised for Christian purposes. The earliest recognisable form of Coptic (datable to the end of the first century AD) was used to write native magical texts, where the motive for the use of the Greek letters probably lay, it is thought, in the desire to render as accurately as possible the correct pronunciation of the magical 'words of power'. In 'Old Coptic', as it is called, the Greek letters are supplemented by several more demotic characters than are retained in the later standardised form of the script.

The surviving literature in Coptic is extensive, with a huge quantity, coming mostly from the libraries of monasteries, being devoted to religious, mainly Biblical, subjects. Non-religious material, much of it again originating from monastic communities, includes private and official correspondence and administrative, business and legal documents, but very little of a purely 'literary' or scientific nature. Most of the surviving texts were written in ink, again with the reed pen, on papyrus or ostraca, though wooden tablets, parchment and, later, paper were also utilised, and the script was adapted without difficulty for monumental use. Many of the documents are in the form of the 'codex', the ancestor of the modern book, made up of individual leaves of papyrus or

32 Coptic ostracon: a pastoral letter from a bishop. Thebes. 6th century AD. H. 13 cm. BM 32782.

33 Wooden lintel from a Coptic church with (left) invocation to 'The Lord Jesus Christ' for the blessed Jōkim and his wife. The damaged text on the right bears the date AD 914. L. 1.93 m. BM 54040.

parchment connected at the spine, which was introduced during the early centuries AD. Whatever the text or format the arrangement and direction of Coptic writing follow the common Greek mode. It is written or carved in horizontal lines reading from left to right. No gaps were left between words and punctuation was minimal (if present at all). A feature peculiar to Sahidic Coptic was the use of a superlinear stroke, unknown to Greek, which was regularly placed above certain consonants or groups of consonants to indicate a syllable.

Literacy

Although it is clear from the quantity and range of the extant record that writing played an immensely important part in ancient Egyptian society, it is very unlikely that literacy can have been widespread among the population. The production of writing, and direct access to it, was almost certainly the preserve of an educated élite, consisting, at the highest level, of royalty and high officials of state and, below them, of people for whom the ability to read and write was a necessary part of their job. There is no doubt that the routine exercise of literacy was largely a function of the professional scribe, who was a central figure in every aspect of the country's administration – civil, military and religious. 21

Recent estimates, admitted to be no more than informed guesses, suggest that less than 1 per cent of the population would have been literate during most of the Pharaonic Period, rising to about 10 per cent in the Graeco-Roman Period, when Greek was the official language of Egypt. Within this generality, allowance must, of course, be made for considerable local variation deriving from special circumstances, such as existed, for example, in the village of Deir el-Medina, the home of the community of workmen who built and decorated the royal tombs at Thebes during the New Kingdom. Draughtsmanship and writing played such an important part in the daily work of these men that they were probably significantly more literate than the general populace. Among the latter, literacy, if it existed at all, is likely to have been restricted to the ability to write one's name and probably not much more. An illiterate person, requiring a document to be written or read, would simply have had recourse to a scribe.

Egyptian writings on the subject indicate that literacy was a very desirable acquisition, conferring status, securing a position and providing a means to advancement that might lead ultimately to the very highest office. A thorough training in scribal skills was held to be an essential prerequisite for any young man with professional or political aspirations. There appear to have been elementary schools at which the basic skills were taught; more advanced training was obtained actually in the job, the system being akin to that of 'apprentice' and 'master', the latter in many cases being a father or near-relative.

School texts of the New Kingdom, which form the bulk of our evidence on Egyptian educational methods, indicate that basic reading and writing were laboriously learned by copying out excerpts from well-known 'classics', at first in cursive hieroglyph and then in the hieratic script. Countless such excerpts survive, written in schoolboy hands

34 Limestone ostracon, the largest of its kind, bearing a copy in school-boy hieratic of part of 'The Story of Sinuhe'. Nineteenth Dynasty. H. 88.5 cm. Ashmolean Museum, Oxford.

of varying competence, on scraps of papyrus, wooden tablets or, most commonly, on limestone ostraca. One of the most famous is the Ramesside ostracon, the largest of its 34 kind, which bears a copy of a sizeable portion of a well-known literary text of the Middle Kingdom, 'The Story of Sinuhe'. Like most efforts of this type, it is a poor version of the text. It contains, in the words of the modern editor of the ostracon, 'every kind of mistake – misspellings, confused constructions, and senseless interpolations – which show that its writer did not know, and suggest that he and his instructors did not care, what the words that he was writing meant'. At a higher level pupils progressed to writing texts actually designed for the purpose of training scribes. Such documents are often cast in the form of letters written by one scribe to another and deliberately include strange words, foreign names, technical terms and difficult calculations – all designed to test the pupil thoroughly. A fine example on a papyrus in the British Museum is devoted 35 to one of the favourite themes of such literature: the advantages of the scribal life as compared to alternatives, in this case military conscription. It is executed in a good literary hand, probably that of an advanced student. The three groups written above the main text are thought to be corrections by the instructor of signs that he felt to be not quite properly formed. The passage begins, 'Apply yourself to writing zealously; do not stay your hand ...', and ends, 'Pleasant and wealth-abounding is your palette and your roll of papyrus'.

35 Advanced exercise in hieratic, including a passage extolling the scribal life. The instructor's corrections are written above. Nineteenth Dynasty. Papyrus Anastasi 5. H. of sheet, approx. 21 cm. BM 10244,4.

3
The Principles

The Egyptian writing system may be regarded as containing three major types of sign, each of which performs a different function. The first type is the 'logogram', which writes a complete word; the second is the 'phonogram', which represents a sound (a phoneme of the language); the third is the 'determinative', which helps to indicate a word's precise meaning. More broadly, since the logogram and the determinative are both concerned with 'sense' or 'meaning' rather than with 'sound', they can be classed together as 'semograms' (or more traditionally, and less adequately, as 'ideograms'). In the nature of the system there is a certain amount of overlap between the categories, and it is not always easy in practice to distinguish clearly between a semographic and a phonographic usage. Moreover, 'there are degrees and varieties within the groups of sense-signs and sound-signs'. The conventional three-fold division of the system presented here covers the essential ground and provides a useful working model, but it should be kept in mind that the categories are not absolutely hard and fast.

An important feature of the system, seen also in scripts of the Semitic branch, is that it records only the consonantal phonemes; the vowels are not specifically indicated. One of the chief characteristics of both the Egyptian and the Semitic languages is that they contain basic word-roots made up of consonants (usually three in number) that are generally invariable; within these roots such features as grammatical inflexion are often indicated by internal vowel variation. It is thought that the neglect of the vowels in writing is a direct reflection of their 'instability' in relation to the consonants.

By the time of Middle Egyptian there were twenty-four consonants in the language. A complete list is given below under 'uniconsonantal signs'. To render their phonemic values Egyptologists are accustomed to transliterate them, as far as is possible, into modern alphabetic characters, some with additional points or marks written above or below (so-called 'diacritics') to differentiate them.

Logograms

The simplest form of logogram is that in which a word is represented directly by a picture of the object that it actually denotes:

⊙ , depicting the sun, signifies 'sun' (r^c)

▭ , depicting the ground-plan of a house, signifies 'house' (pr)

😊 , depicting the human face, signifies 'face' ($ḥr$)

A more developed form works through a kind of extension or association of meaning:

⊙ , depicting the sun, signifies 'day' (r^c or hrw)

🖋 , depicting writing equipment, signifies 'scribe' or 'writing' ($sẖ$)

∧ , depicting a pair of legs, signifies 'come' (iw)

It is clear that a writing system based entirely on such logograms would be quite impractical. Firstly it would require many thousands of signs to cover the vocabulary of a language. Secondly it would find it very difficult to express, clearly and unambiguously, words for things that cannot easily be pictured. It is these considerations, scholars suggest, that, early on, led to the development of the second category of sign, the phonogram.

Phonograms

These were derived by a process of phonetic borrowing, whereby logograms were used to write other words, or parts of words, to which they were unrelated in meaning but with which they happened to share the same consonantal structure. For example:

the logogram ⟨⟩, *r*, meaning 'mouth', was used as a phonogram with the phonemic value *r*, to write such words as ⟨⟩, *r*, meaning 'towards' or to represent the phonemic element *r* in a word like ⟨⟩, *rn*, 'name'.

the logogram ⟨⟩, *pr*, meaning 'house', was used as a phonogram with the value *pr*, in words such as ⟨⟩, *pr*, 'go', or ⟨⟩, *prt*, 'winter'.

the logogram ⟨⟩, *ḥr*, meaning 'face', was used as a phonogram with the value *ḥr*, in such words as ⟨⟩, *ḥr*, 'upon', and ⟨⟩, *ḥrt*, 'sky'.

The basic principle at work here is that of the *rebus*, whereby 'one thing is shown, but another meant'. By the same principle the English verb 'can' could be written with the picture ⟨⟩, representing a (tin) can, or the word 'belief' with the pictures ⟨⟩, representing a bee and a leaf. Using this method the Egyptians were able to develop a large corpus of phonographic signs which was more than adequate to meet their linguistic needs. These phonograms fall naturally into three main categories.

1. Uniconsonantal signs, which represent a single consonant; the most important group. There are twenty-six of these including variants:

Sign	Translit.	Sound-value	Sign	Translit.	Sound-value
	ꜣ	glottal stop		ḥ	emphatic h
	i	i		ḫ	ch as in Scottish loch
	y	y		ẖ	slightly softer than last
	ꜥ	gutteral, the ayin of the Semitic languages		s	s
	w	w		š	sh
	b	b		ḳ	q
	p	p		k	k
	f	f		g	hard g
	m	m		t	t
	n	n		ṯ	tj
	r	r		d	d
	h	h		ḏ	dj

Among these, 𓄿, 𓇋, and 𓏲 are weak consonants. They were readily assimilated in speech to a preceding vowel, especially at the end of a syllable, and consequently were often omitted in writing; the consonant ⌢ was similarly unstable. Egyptologists sometimes indicate the graphic omission of a consonant by enclosing its transliteration in brackets.

2. Biconsonantal signs, which represent pairs of successive consonants; the largest single group of phonograms, though fewer than a hundred in all. We have already encountered ☐, pr, and 𓉐, ḥr. Here are some others:

Sign	Translit.	Sign	Translit.	Sign	Translit.
	ꜣw		mn		sꜣ
	ꜣb or mr		mr		sw
	ir		mr or ꜣb		sn
	wꜣ		ms		šs
	wp		nb		kꜣ
	wr		ns		ti
	wḏ		ḥm		ḏꜣ
	bꜣ		ḫn		dd

3. Triconsonantal signs, which represent groups of three successive consonants. There are between forty and fifty of these, the following being among the most common:

Sign	Transliteration	Sign	Transliteration
	iwn		rwḏ
	ꜥnḫ		ḥtp
	ꜥḥꜥ		ḫpr
	wꜣḥ		ḫrw
	nfr		šmꜥ
	nṯr		tyw
	nḏm		ḏꜥm

It should be noted that although the signs in the last two categories do occur as individual hieroglyphs, they are more often accompanied by uniconsonantal signs, which record part or even the whole of their phonemic value. This is referred to as 'phonetic complementing'. In general it is a single consonant, more usually the last of the group, that is complemented:

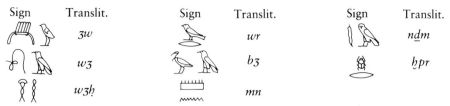

Sign	Translit.	Sign	Translit.	Sign	Translit.
	ȝw		*wr*		*nḏm*
	wȝ		*bȝ*		*ḫpr*
	wȝḥ		*mn*		

Fuller complementing is, however, by no means rare:

Sign	Translit.	Sign	Translit.	Sign	Translit.
	bȝ		*nfr*		*ḥtp*
	ʿnḫ		*ns*		*ḫpr*

The original function of such complements was to emphasise that the complemented sign was indeed a phonogram and not a logogram, but they were also exploited as calligraphic devices, to be deployed, for example, when there was a need to fill an unwanted space.

In theory, the system allowed a word of more than one consonant to be written in a number of different ways. In practice, however, a degree of economy was excercised, with the full range of possibilities being left unexploited and with spellings being relatively standardised. Thus, for example, the preposition *ḥnʿ*, 'together with', is always written and never as ; the verb *mn*, 'to remain', always takes the form or the like, and is never written as ; the adjective *nfr*, 'good', though written variously as , , or , never lacks the triconsonantal ; and the biconsonantals and , though they can both represent *mr*, are used each in a particular set of words (related by root) and are not interchangeable. Many words do have variant forms but their orthography has a sufficiently consistent 'core' to make them recognisable without undue difficulty. This process of word recognition is further aided by the third major category of sign, the determinative.

Determinatives

Determinatives, which like phonograms were derived from logograms, were placed at the end of words to assist in establishing their meaning, where otherwise there might be uncertainty. For example, a determinative in the form of a stroke was commonly appended to a logogram to emphasise that its function was logographic: , 'sun', , 'face', , 'house'. Similarly, to remove ambiguity, a sign or group of signs subject to more than one interpretation would be written with the determinative appropriate to the intended meaning. Thus the logogram , *sš*, would be written , with the determinative depicting a man, when the word 'scribe' was meant, and , with the determinative representing a book-roll, when the word 'write' or 'writing' was meant. We have already noted in Chapter 2 the use of determinatives (in the form of male and female figures) to disambiguate names. So also with other phonograms. For example, the group , *mn*, could stand for a number of different words, among them 'remain' and 'weak'. To distinguish between them, the former was written ⌐⌐⌐⌐‖ , with the book-roll determinative (indicating an abstract notion), the latter ⌐⌐⌐⌐🦅 , with the determinative of a small bird (indicating something small, bad or weak).

Some determinatives are specific in application, which means that they are closely tied to one word:

𓅂 ⊖ 𓎛	*3sḫ*	'to reap'	(determinative of a man reaping)
𓏤𓏤 𓅂 ⌒ 𓃗	*ssmt*	'horse'	(determinative of a horse)

Others identify a word as belonging to a certain class or category. These are called 'generic determinatives' or 'taxograms'. The following form a small selection:

𓀀	man, person	𓂾	walk, run	𓋏	metal
𓁐	woman	𓄹	limb, flesh	⊗	town, village
𓀭	god, king	𓄜	skin, mammal, leather	𓈉	desert, foreign country
𓀡	force, effort	🦅	small, bad, weak	𓉐	house, building
𓀁	eat, drink, speak	⤳	wood, tree	⌐⌐	book, writing, abstract
𓀢	enemy, foreigner	⊙	sun, light, time	I I I	several, plural
⌐▭	force, effort	▭	stone		

Words could be written with one determinative or more:

𓏲 ⌒ 𓅂 ⌐	*ikm*	'shield' ('shield' determinative)
🦅 ▭ 𓀁	*wšb*	'answer' ('speak' determinative)
🦅 ▫𓏲 ⌐▭	*wgs*	'cut open' ('knife' and 'force' determinatives)
𓂾⌒ 🦅 𓀀 𓏪	*bḫ3w*	'fugitives' ('legs', 'man' and 'plural' determinatives)

The determinatives of a word could also be changed or varied, so as to indicate a nuance of meaning. Take the word *ikm*. It is often followed by the specific determinative as above, but it was also written with the leather or metal determinatives (𓄜, 𓋏), when it was felt to be important to distinguish its material. The information conveyed by the determinative in either case is additional to that which is implicit in the word *ikm* itself. It is a special attribute of the Egyptian system that it could convey by pictorial means extra-linguistic information of this kind.

As well as performing a semantic function, determinatives were useful aids to reading. Since they mark the ends of words, they would have helped the reader to identify the 'word-images' or 'word-pictures' in a continuous text. Such 'images' once established were very slow to change, resulting in a stability for the system which certainly had its advantages but which was also one of the major reasons for the gradual divergence between the written and spoken forms of the language (a divergence already well advanced, it is believed, by the time of the Middle Kingdom). As the one failed to keep pace with the other, the script became increasingly 'historical', with a somewhat fossilised orthography no longer accurately reflecting contemporary pronunciations.

As any routine line of inscription will demonstrate, all the categories of sign mentioned above occur regularly, side by side, in Egyptian writing, sometimes together with other, less important, types, called 'orthograms' and 'calligrams', which convey neither meaning nor sound but may be present for special orthographic or aesthetic reasons:

wd ḥm.f ḥr wrryt.f nt dˤm ib.f ʒw

'His Majesty departed upon his chariot of electrum, his heart joyful'

In this line the signs ⵙ (*w*), ⵗ (*f*), ⵖ (*r*), ⵙⵙ (*y*), ⵡⵡ (*n*), ⵔ (*t*), and ⵙ (*m*) are uniconsonantal, with ⵙ (in both cases), ⵗ, and ⵙ, acting as phonetic complements; ⵗ (*wd*), ⵗ (*ḥm*), ⵗ (*ḥr*), ⵙ (*wr*), and ⵗ (*ʒw*) are biconsonantal; ⵗ (*dˤm*) is triconsonantal; ⵗ (*ib* = 'heart') is a logogram; the first ⵗ is an orthogram; and ⵗ, ⵗ, ⵗ, ⵗ, and ⵗ are determinatives.

Such apparent complexity has led the Egyptian system (and others like it) to be treated rather disparagingly by many commentators. Dismissing it as 'cumbrous' and 'illogical', they have found it difficult to understand 'the process of thought by which it was evolved, and even more difficult to imagine why it should have continued with so little development over so long a period'. The central complaint is that the Egyptians, evidently lacking in imagination, failed to take what is deemed to be the 'obvious step': simply to use their uniconsonantal signs in the manner of an alphabet, abandoning the other types of sign. Such criticism, which is based essentially on the assumed superiority of alphabetic scripts over all others, is quite misplaced. It not only overrates the efficiency of alphabetic systems, it also seriously undervalues the merits of others. The Egyptian system has the 'disadvantage' of containing a relatively large number of signs. In compensation, however, its mixed orthography creates visually distinctive word patterns that actually enhance legibility. Direct support for this view is provided by those few attempts at 'alphabetic' writing, which were carried out, perhaps experimentally under the influence of Greek, during Egypt's Late Period. The experiment, if such it was, was short-lived and it is not hard to see why. These 'alphabetic' texts, consisting of a succession of consonantal signs, written in unbroken sequence like Greek of the time, are very difficult to read, considerably more so than contemporary inscriptions written in the traditional orthography. The verdict of one percipient authority is that 'writing Egyptian with only an alphabet of consonants sacrificed legibility to simplicity, and thus did more harm than good ... Perhaps it is now time to stop chiding the Egyptians for not "taking the step which seems to us so obvious"'.

There is, of course, a further dimension to the matter. The reduction of the system in the way suggested would have meant the abandonment of what was evidently to the Egyptians an exceedingly important attribute of the script: namely, its capacity, because of its pictorial and unrestricted nature, to be exploited for purposes other than straightforward linguistic communication. Some of the ways in which the hieroglyphs functioned as part of a larger system of artistic representation were mentioned in the previous chapter, where certain non-scriptorial uses and significances were also noted, while earlier in this chapter attention was drawn to the script's ability to convey 'extralinguistic' information. It is relevant to add here the way in which the script could be manipulated to produce so-called 'sportive' or 'cryptographic' writings, designed, it has been suggested, 'to clothe a religious text in mystery' or simply 'to intrigue the reader'. The extent to which such manipulation was possible is shown most strikingly by the systems of orthography employed in certain temple inscriptions of the Ptolemaic and Roman Periods. They are characterised, among other things, by an enormous increase in the number of signs and variants, in the values and meanings that the signs could bear, and in the possible combinations of signs and sign-groups, an elaboration achieved not by artificial means but simply by exploiting to the full the inherent properties of the hieroglyphic script. To a reader accustomed only to the classical orthography these texts are unintelligible, though it is now doubted that they were actually designed to be deliberately cryptographic. Whatever the reason for such elaboration, it is clear that it was not an original invention of the Ptolemaic Period. On the contrary, it was the final stage of a tradition that is strongly in evidence already in the New Kingdom and can be traced back sporadically as far as the Old Kingdom. Indeed some 'sportive' writings are to be found as regular components of the standard system from a relatively early date. A prime example is the common occurrence, from the Middle Kingdom on, of the hieroglyph ⟍, as an abbreviated writing of the title ⟨hieroglyphs⟩ *imy-r*, 'overseer'. The basis of the usage, which is a 'kind of graphic pun', becomes clear, when it is understood that ⟍ represents a tongue and that the title *imy-r* means literally 'he who is in the mouth'.

Vocalisation

The general absence of vowel notation means that our modern transliterations represent only the consonantal skeletons of Egyptian words. Many of these are difficult to communicate verbally, being, as they stand, virtually unpronounceable. As an aid, therefore, to pronunciation (in discussion, lectures, teaching), Egyptologists insert a short 'e' between the consonants and render ꜣ and ꜥ as 'a'. Thus, for example:

sꜣ	'sa'	*ḥnꜥ*	'hena'
wrs	'weres'	*ꜥḏꜥ*	'adja'
mn	'men'	*nfrt*	'nefret'
wbn	'weben'	*sḥtp*	'sehetep'

It must always be borne in mind, however, that the resulting vocalisations are artificial devices serving as a convenience and bear little or no relation to the ancient pronunciation of the words.

Our knowledge of the original pronunciation of Egyptian is very incomplete but not a total blank. The vocalic structure of a considerable number of words can be deduced from their form in Coptic, the last stage of Egyptian and the only stage in which the vowels are written. Although Coptic contains a large number of Greek and other foreign words, the bulk of its vocabulary is of Pharaonic ancestry, in many cases going back to the earliest stages of the language. A selection is given below of some common Egyptian words together with their Coptic descendants:

	mn (remain)	ⲙⲟⲩⲛ	(moun)
	mdw (speak)	ⲙⲟⲩⲧⲉ	(moute)
	pḏt (bow)	ⲡⲓⲧⲉ	(pite)
	nfr (good)	ⲛⲟⲩϥⲉ	(nūfe)
	r(m)ṯ (man)	ⲣⲱⲙⲉ	(rōme)

(sun disk signs)	*r'* (sun)	ⲣⲏ	(rē)
(hieroglyph signs)	*sf* (yesterday)	ⲥⲁϥ	(saf)
(hieroglyph signs)	*kmt* (Egypt)	ⲕⲏⲙⲉ	(kēme)

The Coptic forms cannot, of course, be accepted as accurate indications of the way in which the words were actually pronounced in earlier periods. Coptic is the end product of centuries, even millennia, of linguistic evolution, in the course of which the grammar of Egyptian, including its phonology, was subject to constant modification and change. One has only to consider that Coptic is separated from Old Egyptian by over 2,000 years – a span of time that is twice as long as that which covers the evolution of modern English from Anglo-Saxon – to realise the potential for change. Coptic is the single most important source of information on the Egyptian vocalic system but its evidence must be used with caution.

There are other, earlier sources of evidence on the subject. A number of ancient scripts (for example, Greek, Assyrian, Babylonian), which themselves indicate vowels, contain fully vocalised transcriptions of contemporary Egyptian words. Such evidence is invaluable, though unfortunately it is very limited in quantity and scope. The earliest and most important of these transcriptions occur in cuneiform documents contemporary with the New Kingdom in Egypt. They include the names of several Egyptian kings, among them such well known ones as *'Imn-ḥtp* (Amenophis) and *R'-mss* (Ramesses), which are transcribed as *Amanhatpi* and *Riamesesa* respectively.

Such vocalisations coupled with careful inferences from the Coptic evidence have enabled scholars to make considerable headway in ascertaining the rules governing Egyptian syllabic structure and vowel quantity and even to get some idea of the quality of the vowels. The indications are that up to the Eighteenth Dynasty Egyptian had only three vowels, namely 'a', 'i' and 'u', all of which could be either long or short. The vowels 'e' and 'o' were relatively late developments.

It should be mentioned at this point that some scholars disagree with the conventional view, followed above, that the phonograms are essentially consonantal. They argue that these signs are really syllabic, standing, in the case of the 'uniconsonantal' signs, for consonant + any vowel. The question is too complex to consider in detail here. Suffice it to say that the 'syllabic' interpretation fits very well with current theories on script development, but is problematic in other respects and is generally rejected by Egyptologists. This theory should not, incidentally, be confused with the phenomenon referred to in Egyptological literature as 'syllabic orthography', also called 'group writing'. This is a method of writing characterised, among other things, by the use of biconsonantal signs, or pairs of uniconsonantal signs, instead of single uniconsonantal signs (for example,⟨sign⟩, *'3*, for *'*; ⟨signs⟩, *h3*, for *h*). In such groups the second element is often a weak consonant indicating the presence of a vowel. Employed mostly to write words of foreign origin, this kind of orthography was particularly popular during the New Kingdom, when its wider usage may have been encouraged by the example of the contemporary cuneiform system, employed very generally throughout Western Asia, in which the vowels are recorded.

Origins

Although the principles underlying Egyptian writing are now fairly well understood, it is still unclear how the system came into being in the first place. Was it the end-product of a process of gradual development or was it the invention of a single person? Was it indigenous or was it introduced from abroad? It is impossible to give definitive answers to these questions. All that can be said in the present state of knowledge is that some alternatives seem more probable than others. Unfortunately, the Egyptians themselves give us no direct help on the subject of the origin of their script. Hieroglyphic writing was traditionally regarded by them as the invention of the gods, in particular of Thoth, the divine scribe, who is often referred to in texts as the 'lord of writing'. We are left to deduce what we can, therefore, from the evidence provided by the earliest examples of the script itself.

Writing makes its first appearance in Egypt at the very end of the Predynastic Period, in the reigns of the immediate predecessors of the kings of the First Dynasty. That it should do so at this time is not altogether surprising. It was a period of great cultural change and technological innovation, with a system of government increasingly concentrated around the royal court. It is reasonable to see writing, within this context, as itself a new technology, invented, or adopted, in response to the needs of the system; the ways in which it was used suggest that it served to further central control both ideologically and administratively.

To the ideological category belong those inscriptions that occur on a series of votive objects decorated with representations in low relief – the first examples of Egyptian 'monumental' art. The most famous of these objects is the palette of King Narmer, in which the king is represented engaged in acts symbolic of his status and authority. The administrative function is to be seen in those labels or dockets usually written in ink, or roughly incised, on the outsides of stone and pottery vessels. The inscriptions in both contexts are short and restricted. They consist almost wholly of titles and names (personal, mainly royal, names, place-names and the names of commodities). In the case of the vessels they identify the owner, the contents and sometimes the source. In the case of the ornamental objects, where the hieroglyphs form an integral part of a larger scene, they identify the representations with which they are associated – the unity between 'caption' and 'figure' in these latter, carefully carved cases, showing clearly how in style and form the hieroglyphs were direct offshoots of the new pictorial art of the period.

Few of these early inscriptions are completely unambiguous. It is not simply a matter of unfamiliar vocabulary. The signary itself had yet to stabilise into its standard dynastic form. It contains several hieroglyphs that do not survive into later usage and whose reading, therefore, can only be guessed at. What is clear, however, is that the basic 'mixed' structure of the writing system is already fully formed – it consists not only of logograms but of phonograms as well; moreover, all the different types of phonogram (uni- and multi-consonantal signs) are present. Thus, for example, among the signs that can be definitely identified on the pottery vessel, the Horus-bird, 🦅, denoting the king as 'the Horus' is a logogram, while 🐦, ⟨, and □ are phonograms, the last two uniconsonantal (i and p), the first triconsonantal ($\check{s}m^c$). In the case of the palette, in addition to what is traditionally regarded as a *rebus* writing the king's name, Narmer (the two hieroglyphs, ⟨catfish⟩, and ⟨chisel⟩, one depicting a cat-fish, the other a chisel, supplying the phonetic values n^cr and mr respectively), there are, among others, the phonograms ⟨⟩, w^c and ⟨⟩, $\check{s}$, quite possibly writing a name $w^c\check{s}$ and ⟨⟩, t, and ⟨⟩, t, combined in what is probably an abbreviated writing of the title t_3ty, 'vizier'. In short, although it was to be some considerable time before its potential was fully exploited – long continuous texts, for example, are not known before the early Old Kingdom – the writing system, already at its inception or very shortly afterwards, had the capacity to express almost everything that was later to be required of it. Elsewhere in the Near East writing is first

36(a) *Left* Slate palette of King Narmer, obverse. The King is represented as the dominant figure smiting an enemy with a mace, in a pose that was to become part of standard royal iconography. His name, written above him with two hieroglyphs, one depicting a cat-fish, the other a chisel, is enclosed in a rectangular structure called the *serekh*. The other figures in the scene are also labelled. Hierakonpolis. Late Predynastic Period. H. 63 cm. Cairo Museum, JE 32169.

36(b) *Below left* Slate palette of King Narmer, reverse. The King is shown in the upper register engaged in a ritual procession. His name occurs twice, written with the same signs as on the obverse, once in a *serekh*, once without. Other identifiable hieroglyphs are present.

37 *Above* Pottery vessel with ink label in cursive hieroglyphs, now somewhat faded. The intelligible signs include a *serekh* enclosing a king's name possibly to be read as *Ka*, surmounted by a falcon denoting the royal title 'Horus'. To the right are three hieroglyphs, *šm*ʿ, *i* and *p*, which can be read as *ip-šm*ʿ, 'tax of Upper Egypt' or the like. Abydos. Late Predynastic Period. H. 27 cm. BM 35508.

attested in contexts of record-keeping and accounting, and the indications seem to be that it developed gradually out of a system of numerical notation. No such 'prehistory' is convincingly traceable for Egyptian writing. On present evidence, admittedly sparse and possibly very misleading, it appears to come into use almost 'ready-made', as it were.

It is generally thought unlikely that full writing could have been invented independently in more than one place in the ancient Near East. This belief coupled with the apparently sudden appearance of writing in a developed form in Egypt has led to the suggestion that the Egyptian system was borrowed from outside. The areas of Mesopotamia and Elam have been cited as the most likely sources, where in the last quarter or so of the fourth millennium BC a pictographic system, similar in appearance and structure to the hieroglyphic script, was used to write first the Sumerian language and then, a little later, the language known as Proto-Elamite. On present estimates the earliest Sumerian writing appears to ante-date the first hieroglyphs by a century or more. That there was contact between Egypt and these areas is beyond doubt. Mesopotamian and Elamite influences are discernible in a number of features of Egyptian culture during the late Predynastic Period, most clearly in the form of various artistic designs and motifs (the intertwined felines on the reverse of Narmer's palette are a case in point). The importation of writing into Egypt can, therefore, be viewed, it has been suggested, as part of a larger process of cultural transmission.

Reasonable as this hypothesis is, there can be no question of the Egyptian system being a direct borrowing of the Sumerian. One obvious objection is that there is little, if any, discernible overlap between the two sets of signs. The Egyptian signary, though pictographic in character like archaic Sumerian, is clearly derived from indigenous sources. Several of the hieroglyphs depict objects, such as certain kinds of tool and weapon, that are known from the archaeological record to have been in contemporary use in Egypt. Others have representational antecedents among the motifs and designs on painted pottery of the earlier Predynastic Period and among the 'mnemonic' symbols, thought to mark possession or ownership, that occur on pots and implements of the same date. More importantly, although both are mixed systems, their structures are not the same. In the first place, the balance of their 'mix' is different. In the earliest Sumerian logography is predominant. Phonography is present at first to a very limited extent, and takes several centuries to become fully developed. By comparison the earliest Egyptian, as noted above, is a system that already contains a substantial, if not complete, phonographic component, in this respect being considerably more advanced than the contemporary Sumerian. In the second place the basic phonetic unit of the system is different in each case. Sumerian is syllabic; its signs represent syllables of the language, each one consisting either of a vowel or of a consonant plus a vowel. Egyptian, on the other hand, is consonantal; its signs represent only the consonants of the language; the vowels, being 'unstable', are not specifically recorded. These differences are rooted in the structures of the languages that the two scripts represent. They are so fundamental as to be decisive against the theory that one system was simply borrowed from the other. The present consensus is, therefore, that if Egyptian writing is to be regarded as not wholly indigenous and Sumerian is to be seen as somehow influential in its invention, then the influence was imparted through a process of what has been called 'stimulus diffusion'; in other words, Sumerian provided the example or the idea of writing, together with some of its operating principles, not the system itself.

4
A Little Basic Grammar

Egyptian grammar is a large and complicated subject, important areas of which are still imperfectly understood. It cannot, without distortion, be reduced to a series of simple rules. This present chapter is intended merely to give a flavour – to a non-Egyptological readership – of how the language works. It is *highly selective* and is confined to Middle Egyptian, the 'classical' stage of the language and the one with which the study of Egyptian is usually begun. It includes also a brief account of other important topics; numerals, kings' names, dates and the offering formula.

Gender and number

There are two genders in Egyptian, masculine and feminine. Masculine nouns have no special ending; feminine nouns end in △, *t*.

sn 'brother'

snt 'sister'

b3k 'servant'

b3kt '(female) servant'

pr 'house'

nht 'tree'

There are three numbers, singular, plural and dual. The plural endings are 𝔅, *w*, for masculine and 𝔅, *wt*, for feminine, though the 𝔅 is often omitted in writing. The determinative of plurality, written ⵏⵏⵏ or ⵏ is normally present at the end of plural words.

snw 'brothers'

snwt 'sisters'

b3kw 'servants'

b3kwt '(female) servants'

prw 'houses'

nhwt 'trees'

The dual is used for pairs of things. The masculine ending is 𝔅″, *wy*, the feminine is △\\, *ty*:

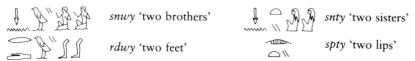

snwy 'two brothers'

snty 'two sisters'

rdwy 'two feet'

spty 'two lips'

Adjectives take their gender and number from the noun they describe and are placed after the noun:

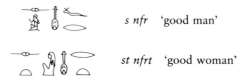

s nfr 'good man'

st nfrt 'good woman'

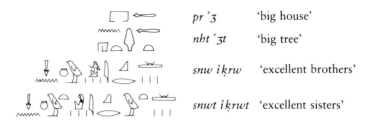

pr ʿꜢ	'big house'
nḫt ʿꜢt	'big tree'
snw iḳrw	'excellent brothers'
snwt iḳrwt	'excellent sisters'

The article and co-ordination

There are no direct equivalents of the English definite and indefinite articles, 'the' and 'a'. Thus, for example, 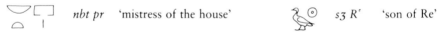, *pr*, may be rendered 'house', 'a house' or 'the house' according to context. Similarly there is no special word for 'and', co-ordination being expressed more often than not by direct juxtapositioning:

sn snt 'brother and sister'

nṯrw nṯrwt 'gods and goddesses'

The cases

Egyptian is not an inflected language, like Latin or German. There are no case-endings to indicate the syntactic function of a noun. Whether a noun is the subject or the object of a verb is indicated by its position in a sentence, the normal word order being verb + noun-subject + noun-object:

(verb) (subject) (object)

sḏm s ḫrw, 'the man hears the voice'

The genitive is expressed in two ways, direct and indirect. In the direct genitive the second noun follows the first without a connecting link. It is thought that in this form the genitive expresses a particularly close relationship:

nbt pr 'mistress of the house' *sꜢ Rʿ* 'son of Re'

In the indirect genitive the second noun is preceded by the genitival adjective 〰〰 , *n(y)*, plural ⊙, *nw*, which agrees in number and gender with the first noun:

	sbꜢ n pr	'door of the house'
	niwt nt nḥḥ	'city of eternity'
	wrw nw Ꜣbḏw	'great ones of Abydos'

When the genitive is pronominal it is expressed by the so-called suffix pronoun, the forms and meanings of which are as follows:

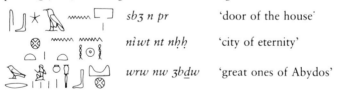

	i	'my'	or	*s*	'her', 'its'
	k	'your' (masculine singular)		*n*	'our'
	t	'your' (feminine singular)		*ṯn*	'your' (plural)
	f	'his'		*sn*	'their'

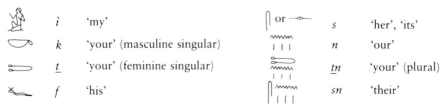

These pronouns serve also as the subject of verbs and the object of prepositions (see below). Note that in transliteration it is customary to place a dot before a suffix.

The dative is rendered simply by means of the preposition ⌇⌇⌇⌇, *n*, 'to' or 'for', which always precedes its object, whether noun or pronoun:

⌇⌇⌇⌇ ▱ ⌷ *n nbt pr* 'for the mistress of the house'　⌇⌇⌇⌇ ⊖ *n.s* 'for her'

Prepositions
The most common prepositions are:

Such phrases are usually placed at the end or towards the end of a clause:

sḏm s ẖrw m pr
'the man hears the voice in the house'

Sentences
Sentence structure and, in particular, the nature and role of the verb, are the most problematic areas of Egyptian grammar. The traditional view is that there are two types of sentence in Egyptian, verbal and non-verbal. Although according to present theory this is not an accurate formulation, it may still serve for the practical purpose of translating Egyptian into English. It is important to note that, in Egyptian, distinctions of 'tense' and 'mood' and the difference between 'main' and 'subordinate' clauses are rarely indicated clearly in the writing and can often only be determined by reference to the context.

In the non-verbal sentence the link between subject and predicate is left unexpressed:

⊖◉ 𓅃 ▱ *rˁ m pt* 'the sun (is, was) in the sky'

▱ 𓀀 𓅃 *nb m pr* 'the master (is, was) in the house'

In the verbal sentence the predicate is a verb, most typically one belonging to the so-called 'suffix-conjugation', the basic pattern of which is verb stem + suffix-pronoun.

Egyptologists refer to it as the *sḏm.f* (sedjemef) form, after the verb traditionally used as the model. The *sḏm.f* is not a simple unity. Owing to the lack of vowel notation, the word as written 'conceals' several different forms, each of which has its own meaning. The most frequently encountered is the 'indicative' *sḏm.f*, which expresses an event as an objective fact. Conventionally translated as a present tense, it is actually 'tenseless', and, depending on context, may have past and future, as well as present, reference. It conjugates as follows:

	sḏm.i	'I hear'		*sḏm.s*	'she, it, hears'
	sḏm.k	'you (masc.) hear'		*sḏm.n*	'we hear'
	sḏm.t	'you (fem.) hear'		*sḏm.tn*	'you hear'
	sḏm.f	'he hears'		*sḏm.sn*	'they hear'

The subject of the verb may also, of course, be a noun, which, like the pronoun, follows the verb, as in the sentence 'the man hears the voice' cited above.

The numerals
The numerals are denoted by seven special signs:

ǀ	*wꜥ*	1		*ḏbꜥ*	10,000
∩	*mḏw*	10		*ḥfnw*	100,000
ϙ	*št*	100		*ḥḥ*	1,000,000
	ḫꜣ	1,000			

When written together to form a single number they are placed in descending order of magnitude. Multiples of each are indicated by simple repetition of the sign:

7 = ǀǀǀǀǀǀǀ   369 =

24 =   142,235 =

The numeral is placed after the noun, which is generally in the singular:

s 7 'seven men'   *niwt ḫꜣ* 'a thousand towns'

The King's names
When a king ascended the throne he assumed five 'great names', the two principal among them being what Egyptologists call the *prenomen* and the *nomen*. These names are easily distinguished because they are enclosed within so-called 'cartouches' or royal rings: . The Egyptian name for the cartouche was , *šnw* (shenu), 'that which encircles'. It is thought that the cartouche symbolised the fact that the bearer of the name ruled over everything that the sun encircles. The *prenomen* is often preceded by the titles , *nṯr nfr*, 'good god', , *nb tꜣwy*, 'lord of the two lands', and, most importantly, , *nswt-bỉty*, 'King of Upper and Lower Egypt', while the *nomen* is introduced by , *sꜣ Rꜥ*, 'son of Re'. Frequently the epithet , *dỉ ꜥnḫ*, 'given life',

or ⟨hieroglyphs⟩, *di ʿnḫ ḏt*, 'given life eternally', follows the names. Here is a titulary featuring the names of Tuthmosis III of the Eighteenth Dynasty:

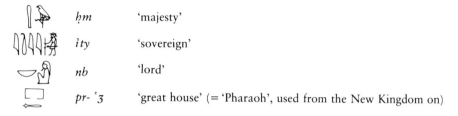

nṯr nfr nb tȝwy nswt-biʾty Mn-ḫpr-Rʿ sȝ Rʿ Ḏḥwty-ms di ʿnḫ ḏt

'The good god, lord of the two lands, king of Upper and Lower Egypt, Men-kheper-Re, son of Re, Tuthmosis, given life eternally'

The ordinary word for king, already encountered above, is *nswt*, ⟨hieroglyphs⟩, often abbreviated to ⟨hieroglyph⟩. Here are some other common designations with their conventional translations:

⟨hieroglyph⟩	*ḥm*	'majesty'
⟨hieroglyph⟩	*iʾty*	'sovereign'
⟨hieroglyph⟩	*nb*	'lord'
⟨hieroglyph⟩	*pr-ʿȝ*	'great house' (= 'Pharaoh', used from the New Kingdom on)

Such designations are often followed by the 'wish formula', ⟨hieroglyphs⟩, *ʿnḫ(w) wḏȝ(w) snb(w)*, 'may he live, be prosperous, be healthy', usually abbreviated to ⟨hieroglyphs⟩.

Dates

Dating in Egypt was not continual but was based on the year of the reigning king. The year was subdivided into seasons, months and days. The full system consists of the following categories:

1. regnal year	⟨hieroglyph⟩	*ḥȝt-sp*	
2. month (four in a season)	⟨hieroglyph⟩	*tpy*	(the first month)
	⟨hieroglyph⟩	*ȝbd*	(the remaining months)
3. season (three in a year)	⟨hieroglyph⟩	*ȝḫt*	(inundation)
	⟨hieroglyph⟩	*prt*	(winter)
	⟨hieroglyph⟩	*šmw*	(summer)
4. day (thirty in a month)	⟨hieroglyph⟩	*sw*	

Here are some typical dates:

⟨hieroglyphs⟩ *ḥȝt-sp 2 ȝbd 3 ȝḫt sw 1*
'year 2, month 3 of the inundation season, day 1' (of the reigning king)

⟨hieroglyphs⟩ *ḥȝt-sp 12 tpy prt sw 11*
'year 12, month 1 of winter, day 11' (of the reigning king)

Commonly, dates are abbreviated giving only the year of the king, as on a stela in the   38
British Museum:

38   Hieroglyphic inscription from a stela mentioning year nineteen of King Nubkaure
     (Ammenemes II). Twelfth Dynasty. BM 583.

ḥȝt-sp 19 *ḫr ḥm n nṯr nfr nswt-bȉty Nbw-kȝw-rˁ*

'year 19 under the majesty of the good god, king of Upper and Lower Egypt, Nub-kau-
re' (Ammenemes II of the Twelfth Dynasty)

The offering formula

A very large number of Egyptian texts, particularly those on funerary stelae, begin with
the hieroglyphs ![glyph], *ḥtp dȉ nswt*, probably to be translated as 'an offering which
the king gives' or similar. It is referred to by Egyptologists as the 'offering formula' or the
'hetep-di-neswt-formula'. A common variant of the formula, ![glyph], *ḥtp dȉ ʾInpw*, 'an
offering which Anubis gives', has already been encountered on the panel of Iry. Its
purpose was to procure for a named beneficiary a perpetual supply of the provisions
deemed necessary for continued existence in the after-life. The underlying idea seems to
have been that the king first provided for the gods, prominent among them ![glyph],
Wsȉr, 'Osiris', and ![glyph], *ʾInpw*, 'Anubis', and that they in turn provided for the
dead person or, more strictly, for the dead person's ⌣, *kȝ*, 'spirit'. In the full writing of
the formula, the provisions invoked from the gods are collectively referred to as ![glyph],
prt-ḫrw, conventionally rendered as 'invocation offerings' and are then individually
itemised. The standard provisions are: ![glyph], *t*, 'bread', ![glyph], *ḥnkt*, 'beer', ![glyph],
kȝw, 'oxen', ![glyph], *ȝpdw*, 'fowl', ![glyph], *šs*, 'alabaster', and ![glyph], *mnḫt*, 'clothing'. The
following is a typical example:

ḥtp dȉ nswt Wsȉr nb Ḏdw nb ȝbdw dȉ.f prt-ḫrw t ḥnkt kȝw ȝpdw šs mnḫt n kȝ n nbt pr Mrrt

'an offering which the king gives (to) Osiris, lord of Busiris, lord of Abydos, that he may
give invocation offerings (consisting of) bread, beer, oxen, fowl, alabaster and clothing,
for the spirit of the mistress of the house, Mereret'

5
Decipherment

The spread of Christianity in Egypt, and the consequent development of the Coptic script, sounded the final death-knell for the ancient 'pagan' writing system. The evidence suggests that by the end of the fifth century AD knowledge of how to read and write the old scripts was extinct. A long dark age – destined to last thirteen centuries and more – descended upon the ancient records. The break in knowledge was complete. The hieroglyphs were fully surrendered to the larger myth of ancient Egypt – the land of strange customs and esoteric wisdom – fostered and handed down by classical writers. Although the Egyptians had been respected throughout classical antiquity as the inventors of writing, this respect does not seem to have been attended by any serious attempt to understand the basic principles of their writing system. The belief that the hieroglyphs, as opposed to the everyday 'popular' script, were not elements of an ordinary writing system but were somehow symbolic and imbued with secret meaning had already become well rooted by the time the historian Diodorus Siculus visited Egypt in the century before Christ: 'their writing does not express the intended concept by means of syllables joined to one another, but by means of the significance of the objects which have been copied, and by its figurative meaning which has been impressed upon the memory by practice.' During the early centuries AD, this 'figurative meaning' received further elaboration. For the influential philosopher Plotinus, writing in the third century, the hieroglyphs were nothing less than Platonic ideas in visual form, 'each picture ... a kind of understanding and wisdom', revealing to the initiated true knowledge as to the essence and substance of things.

Within, and out of, this tradition, there grew a genre of literature specially devoted to the explanation of hieroglyphs. The best preserved and most famous treatise on the subject is the *Hieroglyphika* of Horapollo, which was probably compiled in the fourth or fifth century AD. Here is one of its entries:

> 'What they mean by a vulture
> When they mean a mother, a sight, or boundaries, or foreknowledge ... they draw a vulture. A mother, since there is no male in this species of animal ... the vulture stands for sight since of all other animals the vulture has the keenest vision. . . . It means boundaries, because when a war is about to break out, it limits the place in which the battle will occur, hovering over it for seven days. Foreknowledge, because of what has been said above and because it looks forward to the amount of corpses which the slaughter will provide it for food ...'

There is a germ of truth in this account, in as much as the Egyptian word for 'mother', , *mwt*, is written with the hieroglyph representing a vulture, but the 'explanations', conceived wholly in allegorical terms, are otherwise complete fantasy.

The importance of the *Hieroglyphika*, however, lies not in its content but in the influence that it exerted over the formation and direction of later opinion and research. When, following the Renaissance in Europe, there arose a new curiosity in things Egyptian, the Neoplatonic tradition, embodied in such 'authoritative' ancient sources as Horapollo, encouraged a line of research that was to prove a long blind alley for scholars attempting to elucidate the 'enigmatic' hieroglyphs. A good example of its influence is to be seen in the conclusions reached after years of extensive study by the German polymath Athanasius Kircher (1602–80). A linguist of great ability, Kircher's translations of hieroglyphic texts, based entirely on preconceived notions as to their symbolic functioning, are wholly wide of the mark, to the point of absurdity. One oft-quoted example may suffice. The name of the king Apries written in hieroglyphs was taken by Kircher to mean 'the benefits of the divine Osiris are to be procured by means of sacred ceremonies and of the chain of the Genii, in order that the benefits of the Nile may be obtained'. Despite his mistaken views of the meaning of the hieroglyphs, Kircher, nevertheless, occupies an honourable place in Egyptological history. He was the author of the first Coptic grammar and vocabulary, works that proved to be an enormous stimulus to the development of Coptic studies. Since knowledge of Coptic was to be a vital element in the eventual decipherment of the hieroglyphs, modern Egyptology owes a considerable debt to the pioneering efforts of Kircher in this field.

Though the myth of the secret hieroglyphs was to remain deeply entrenched, the century following Kircher's death saw a generally more cautious approach to their interpretation. While Kircher's translations were wholly rejected, few complete solutions were offered as alternatives. In 1785 the French orientalist C. J. de Guignes (1721–1800), tried to prove the unity of the Egyptian and Chinese scripts, under the false belief that China had been an Egyptian colony. More valuable, and to the point, was his elaboration of an idea first mooted in 1762 by another French scholar, J. J. Barthélemy (1716–95), that the rings or 'cartouches' to be observed frequently in Egyptian texts enclosed royal names. This was the first hint of a breakthrough, but in the state of knowledge then prevailing the means of making further progress were lacking. In due course, following the discovery of the Rosetta Stone, the means became available and the royal cartouche was to prove the very key that unlocked the secrets of the hieroglyphs.

39   The Rosetta Stone was discovered in July, 1799, near the town of Rashid, ancient Rosetta, which is situated in the Delta, on the western arm of the Nile near the sea. It was unearthed, quite fortuitously, by a gang of French soldiers who were part of Napoleon Bonaparte's invading army. Under the command of an officer named Pierre Bouchard, they were digging foundations for a fort and, according to one account, found the monument built into an ancient wall. The 'stone' – a substantial slab of black basalt, 118 cm high, 77 cm wide, 30 cm thick, and weighing 762 kg – is actually a commemorative stela, which was once set up in an Egyptian temple. It is broken and was probably about 50 cm or so higher when intact. Incised on one face, it bears an inscription dated to year 9 of the reign of Ptolemy V Epiphanes, corresponding to 27 March 196 BC, the main part of which is a copy of a decree issued by a general council of Egyptian priests recording the honours bestowed upon the king by the temples of Egypt. The point of crucial importance about the inscription is that it is reproduced in three different scripts: hieroglyphic at the top, demotic in the middle, and Greek at the bottom. None of the sections has escaped damage, the worst affected being the hieroglyphic. The bilingual nature of the text and the potential that this offered, since Greek was a known language, for the decipherment of the Egyptian versions, were immediately apparent to the French *savants* who first examined the stone after its transference to Cairo. To their enormous credit they lost no time in making ink impressions of the inscriptions and in distributing them among the scholars of Europe. After the defeat of Napoleon's army, the stone itself, which had been moved to Alexandria, was ceded to the British in 1801, together with other antiquities, under Article XVI of the Treaty of Alexandria. It was shipped back to Britain in February, 1802, and was deposited for some months at the Society of Antiquaries of London, where a translation of the Greek section was read out in April of that year by the Rev. Stephen Weston and where further reproductions were subsequently made. It was transferred to the British Museum towards the end of 1802, where it remains to the present day.

39 The Rosetta Stone bearing a single text written in three different scripts: hieroglyphic at the top, demotic in the middle, Greek at the bottom. 196 BC. H. 1.18 m. BM 24.

The distribution of the various copies of the stone inaugurated a period of intense study, with scholars competing anxiously and even jealously to be the first to achieve the prize of decipherment. The 'devil of hieroglyphics', as it has been called, was let loose in no uncertain terms. A stream of lectures and publications ensued and new theories and 'solutions' were espoused, most of them hopelessly erroneous and some of them as bizarre as the translations offered by Kircher a century and a half before. In fact the hieroglyphic portion of the stone was to remain intractable for many years more. It was the study of the demotic section, recognised as the 'popular' writing mentioned in ancient Greek sources, that yielded the first positive results.

Already by the end of 1802, before the stone had had time to settle in its new home at the British Museum, two important contributions to the subject had appeared, the first by the French scholar Sylvestre de Sacy (1758–1832), the second by the Swedish diplomat and orientalist, de Sacy's pupil, Johan Åkerblad (1763–1819). The former had decided to concentrate on the demotic section as it was virtually complete, missing only the beginnings of a few lines, whereas the hieroglyphic section was incomplete and was, in any case, a less-promising proposition since 'the hieroglyphic character, being representative of ideas, not sounds, does not belong to the domain of any particular language'. De Sacy's approach to the demotic was eminently sensible. He began with the Greek proper names and attempted to isolate their demotic versions. He believed that this would enable him to identify the values of the demotic letters, which could then be used as stepping stones to further correlations. In practice the process proved to be more difficult than he had anticipated. He met with partial success in isolating the demotic groups for the names of Ptolemy and Alexander, but he found it impossible to identify the values of the individual characters.

Åkerblad, following de Sacy's method, made more substantial progress. He was able to identify in the demotic all the proper names occurring in the Greek, among them, in addition to Ptolemy and Alexander, Arsinoe, Berenice and Aelos. From the sound values thus obtained, he built up a 'demotic alphabet' of twenty-nine letters, almost half of which were actually correct. He then demonstrated that the phonetic signs used to write the names were also used to spell ordinary words, thus providing the first definite indication of the general phonetic character of the demotic script. Among several individual words, apart from names, that he correctly identified are those for 'Greek', 'Egyptian', 'temple', 'love', 'him' and 'his', all of which he was able to correlate with their Coptic equivalents. These were impressive achievements, but, ironically, Åkerblad's very success in establishing the values of so many demotic characters now led him astray. He became convinced that the script was entirely phonetic or 'alphabetic', as he called it. This belief proved an insurmountable barrier to further progress on his part.

After these early successes with the demotic, virtually nothing of value was achieved for another twelve years. Then, at the beginning of 1814, fragments of a papyrus written with 'running Egyptian characters' were submitted for study to the Englishman Thomas Young (1773–1829), a scientist of international distinction and an accomplished linguist. The study of this material aroused his interest in the Rosetta inscriptions and in the summer of that year he began to subject them to the most careful scrutiny. He began, like de Sacy and Åkerblad before, with the demotic or 'epistolographic' as it was also known. Within a few weeks Young had been able to isolate in the demotic most of the graphic groups representing individual words and to relate them to their equivalents in the Greek, but he found it difficult to go further:

> 'You tell me that I shall astonish the world if I make out the inscription. I think it on the contrary astonishing that it should not have been made out already, and that I should find the task so difficult as it appears to be ... by far the greater part of the words I have ascertained with tolerable certainty, and some of the

most interesting without the shadow of a doubt; but I can read very few of them alphabetically, except the proper names which Åkerblad had read before ...'

An important observation was soon to follow, however:

'after having completed this analysis of the hieroglyphic inscription, I observed that the epistolographic characters of the Egyptian inscription, which expressed the words God, Immortal, Vulcan, Priests, Diadem, Thirty, and some others, had a striking resemblance to the corresponding hieroglyphs; and since none of these characters could be reconciled, without inconceivable violence, to the forms of any imaginable alphabet, I could scarcely doubt that they were imitations of the hieroglyphics, adopted as monograms or verbal characters, and mixed with the letters of the alphabet.'

These are the first intimations of two crucially important points: firstly that demotic was not a wholly separate script from hieroglyphic; secondly that the Egyptian system was a mix of different types of character.

In the year or so following, Young spread his researches beyond the Rosetta texts, drawing also on other material, an increasing amount of which was now becoming available. Particularly useful for him were the inscriptions newly published in the volumes of the *Description de l'Égypte* (the scholarly fruits of the Napoleonic expedition) and some unpublished papyri, 'funeral rolls', recently brought from Egypt and placed at his disposal. His eye for significant detail is revealed by his observation that the hieroglyphic group ⌂, which he commonly found attached to what were evidently personal names in the funerary papyri, was in fact a 'female termination', a sound conclusion that was to be of considerable value at a later stage of the decipherment. Even more significantly, by the judicious comparison of parallel texts occurring in the funerary documents, he was able to confirm the relationship of the various Egyptian scripts by tracing the 'degradation from the *sacred* character, through the *hieratic*, into the *epistolographic*, or common running hand of the country'. This conclusion led him on directly to what was to be his single most important contribution to the process of decipherment: the partial subversion of the great myth that the hieroglyphic script was entirely 'symbolic'. Turning back again to the Rosetta texts, he now quickly established the equivalence of many of the demotic and hieroglyphic signs. One of the outcomes of this process was the firm identification of the only personal name that occurs in the hieroglyphic section, that of King Ptolemy. Since the demotic expressed the name phonetically, it was logical to conclude, in Young's view, that the hieroglyphic equivalent did so also.

The name of Ptolemy occurs six times in the hieroglyphic section, three in a short cartouche and three in a longer one:

'Ptolemaios'   'Ptolemaios, may he live for ever beloved of Ptah'

Deducing that the shorter contained the name Ptolemy alone, while the longer contained the name plus title, Young conjectured the phonetic values of the name signs to be as follows:

Hieroglyph	Young Value	Correct Value
□	p	p
⌂	t	t
𓊃	'not essentially necessary'	o

Hieroglyph	Young Value	Correct Value
(glyph)	lo or ole	l
(glyph)	ma or simply m	m
(glyph)	i	i or y
(glyph)	osh or os	s

He followed this with a similar analysis of the name of the Ptolemaic queen, Berenice, which he had isolated, somewhat fortuitously, on a copy of an inscription from the temple of Karnak at Thebes:

Hieroglyph	Young Value	Correct Value
(glyph)	bir	b
(glyph)	e	r
(glyph)	n	n
(glyph)	i	i
(glyph)	'superfluous'	k
(glyph)	ke or ken	a
(glyph)	'feminine termination'	female determinative

These two analyses, with the hieroglyphs treated as phonograms (and four or five of them quite correctly identified), represent an enormous step forward conceptually. The door was now open at last to a real understanding of the largely phonetic nature of the hieroglyphic script. Sadly, at the very threshold, Young's progress came to an abrupt halt. The old myth still exercised a potent influence. Young was convinced that the phonetic principle could only be of limited validity, that the 'hieroglyphic alphabet' was a 'mode of expressing sounds in some particular cases, and not as having been universally employed where sounds were required'. In other words, the hieroglyphs were mostly symbolic; only in special cases, such as in the rendering of foreign names, were they used to represent sounds. Drawing on an analogy from Chinese, he viewed the cartouche surrounding the royal name as a mark denoting that this special process was in operation:

> 'it is extremely interesting to trace some of the steps by which alphabetic writing seems to have arisen out of hieroglyphical; a process which may indeed be in some measure illustrated by the manner in which the modern Chinese express a foreign combination of sounds, the characters being rendered simply 'phonetic' by an appropriate mark, instead of retaining their natural signification; and this mark, in some modern printed books, approaching very near to the ring surrounding the hieroglyphic names.'

The results of Young's researches, of four years' duration in all, were published by him in 1819 in a splendid article entitled 'Egypt' for the *Supplement to the fourth edition of the Encyclopaedia Britannica*. In the years following he continued to work, with intermittent success, on the problems of the hieroglyphs, but he entirely failed to capitalise on his own initial breakthrough. The prize of final decipherment was to fall to another scholar, Young's contemporary and rival, the brilliant young Frenchman, Jean-François Champollion (1790–1832).

The latter's route to the decipherment was also via the name of Ptolemy, the identity of

40 *Right* Jean-François Champollion
(1790–1832). Portrait by Coignet,
1831. Musée du Louvre, Paris.

41 *Below* A plate from Champollion's
Lettre à M. Dacier, published in
1822. Listed are the various demotic
and hieroglyphic signs which form
the Egyptian 'phonetic alphabet'
together with their Greek equivalents.
At the bottom enclosed in a cartouche
is Champollion's name written by
him in demotic.

Pl. IV.

Tableau des Signes Phonétiques
des écritures Hiéroglyphique et Démotique des anciens Égyptiens

Lettres Grecques	Signes Démotiques	Signes Hiéroglyphiques
A		
B		
Γ		
Δ		
E		
Z		
H		
Θ		
I		
K		
Λ		
M		
N		
Ξ		
O		
Π		
P		
Σ		
T		
Υ		
Φ		
Ψ		
X		
Ω		
TΘ		

which he appears to have determined by a similar process of deduction to that of Young. To what extent, if any, Champollion's initial discoveries were dependent on Young's work has long been a matter of dispute. Champollion's famous paper on the phonetic nature of the hieroglyphs, *Lettre à M. Dacier relative à l'alphabet des hiéroglyphes phonétiques*, appeared in 1822, three years after Young's article 'Egypt'. Whether or not Champollion learned anything from Young, it is beyond dispute that he rapidly overtook him. Young's results, though they pointed in the right direction, were limited and inconclusive. Champollion was the first to *prove*, by systematic analysis of the available evidence, that the hieroglyphic script operated on the phonetic principle, and to build on this effectively. Champollion realised that to make real progress it was necessary somehow to isolate a pair of already known names having several hieroglyphs in common. These would act as an independent check on each other and would provide a firm basis for further identifications. In early 1822, by a happy chance, a copy of another bilingual inscription containing just such a pair of names came into his hands.

In 1819 the English traveller, W. J. Bankes, had transported back from Egypt to his home in Kingston Lacy, Dorset, an obelisk and its base block, which had once stood in the temple of Philae near Aswan. On the base was a Greek inscription mentioning two royal names, Ptolemy and Cleopatra, while on the obelisk itself was a hieroglyphic text including two different cartouches. Bankes inferred from the Greek that the cartouches contained the names of Ptolemy and Cleopatra and noted that the hieroglyphs in one corresponded exactly to those in the cartouche on the Rosetta Stone identified as Ptolemy by Young. In 1821 Bankes had a lithograph made of both the Greek and hieroglyphic texts, copies of which, annotated by Bankes with the suggested identifications of the names, were widely distributed. For Champollion the receipt of one of these copies was, in the words of one commentator, 'the moment which … turned bewildering investigation into brilliant and continuous decipherment'.

Omitting the epithets accompanying the name of Ptolemy and the signs representing the 'female termination' in the other, the cartouches on the Bankes' obelisk read so:

Ptolemaios   Cleopatra

Champollion identified the values of the individual signs as follows:

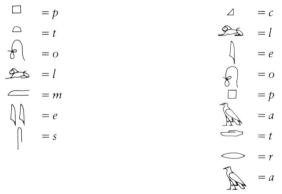

There was an encouraging degree of correspondence between the signs which occurred in both names. Only the ◠ and ⊂▭ did not correlate but for this Champollion had a ready explanation. He deduced correctly that the two signs were actually 'homophones' – separate signs that could represent the same value, here a *t*.

Champollion knew that if these identifications were correct it should be possible to apply the values gained from the names of Ptolemy and Cleopatra to other cartouches and to produce further recognisable names. This he now proceeded to do, beginning with the cartouche:

From the known values the following elements could be identified:

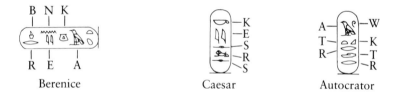

When the range of possible names was considered, it was not difficult to fill the gaps with *k*, *n*, and *s* to yield the name *alksentrs* = Greek Alexandros (Alexander), with ⌒, ∿∿∿, ─◦─ identified as *k*, *n* and *s* respectively, the first and last understood as homophones for ⊿ and ∩. By the extension of this method there quickly followed further identifications, including the name of Queen Berenice (confirming and correcting Young's suggestions) and the names and titles of several Roman emperors:

B N K
| | |

R E A

Berenice

K
E
S
R
S

Caesar

A— —W
T— —K
R— —T
—R

Autocrator

It seems that during at least the initial stages of the decipherment Champollion had believed, like Young, that the phonetic system operated only for the expression of foreign names and elements of the Graeco-Roman Period. It was to these that his *Lettre à M. Dacier*, published in late 1822, was largely devoted. At the end of the *Lettre*, however, he announced an entirely new and astonishing discovery: the phonetic system was of wider application and could be extended back into earlier times. The final breakthrough had been achieved.

It appears that in September 1822 Champollion had received copies of various reliefs and inscriptions from Egyptian temples. One of them, from the temple of Abu Simbel in Nubia, contained cartouches enclosing a name repeated in a variety of ways but in its simplest form as . The last two signs were familiar to him from the cartouches of the Graeco-Roman rulers as bearing the phonetic value *s*. But what of the first two signs? Champollion had an excellent knowledge of Coptic and here it came fully into play. The first hieroglyph appeared to represent the sun, for which the Coptic word was ⲢH (*rē*). Supplying this value for the first hieroglyph produced the sequence

$Re + ? + s + s$. There immediately sprung to Champollion's mind the combination $Re + m + s + s$ yielding the well-known name Rameses or Ramesses, identified as a king of the Nineteenth Dynasty in the history (written in Greek) of the Ptolemaic historian, Manetho. By this analysis, the sign 𓏠 should logically be accorded the value m. More evidence was at hand. A second sheet of drawings included the cartouche ⬭. Here again was the group 𓏠𓏤 already conjectured to be $m + s$, in this case preceded by a hieroglyph that Champollion recognised as the picture of an ibis, known to be the symbol of the god Thoth. Surely the name was none other than Thoth-mes, the Tuthmosis of Manetho's Eighteenth Dynasty. For confirmation of the value of 𓏠 Champollion was able to turn to the Rosetta Stone, where the sign occurs, again in conjunction with 𓏤, as part of a group corresponding to the Greek *genethlia*, 'birth day', which at once suggested to Champollion the Coptic word for 'give birth', ⲙⲓⲥⲉ (mīse). It should be noted that Champollion was actually in error in interpreting 𓏠 as having the value m. It does, in fact, have the value ms, being a biconsonantal sign to which 𓏤 had been added as a phonetic complement. At this stage, understandably, Champollion was unaware of the possibility of multiconsonantal signs. Fortunately the error was not crucial.

Champollion published these and many other subsequent discoveries in his *Précis du système hiéroglyphique* (1824), a work in which he conclusively demonstrated that the phonetic principle, far from being of limited application, was, as he called it, the 'soul' of the entire writing system. For the first time the true relationship between the semograms and the phonograms, including the function of the determinative, was revealed. In addition a huge quantity of new data was presented and identified – royal, private and divine names, titles and epithets, as well as ordinary vocabulary. Furthermore there was grammatical analysis and translation of phrases and sentences. Inevitably there were mistakes, but the fundamental approach was absolutely sound. With the appearance of the *Précis*, the ancient myth of the hieroglyphs was finally laid to rest and the science of Egyptology was born.

6
Borrowings

No account of the hieroglyphic script would be complete without some consideration of its contribution to the writing of languages other than Egyptian. The other great writing system of the ancient Near East, cuneiform, was adapted through the course of three millennia to write a large variety of languages. By comparison the Egyptian contribution was small but was not completely insignificant. Some scholars believe that the example of Egyptian hieroglyphs may well have stimulated the development of Cretan and Hittite 'hieroglyphs' in the first half of the second millennium BC. More certainly, in the case of two other scripts – Protosinaitic and Meroïtic – there was the direct borrowing of Egyptian signs.

Protosinaitic

Protosinaitic is a script that was initially noted in various localities in the Sinai peninsula, hence its name. Serious attention was first drawn to it in 1906 by the British archaeologist, Flinders Petrie (1853–1942), following his expedition to Sinai where he explored the sites of the turquoise mines worked anciently by the Egyptians. The most important of these sites, Serabit el-Khadim, bore the remains of a temple dedicated to Hathor, the chief goddess of the Sinai mining area. It was here that Petrie made his most substantial discoveries, including a large number of inscriptions, many dedicated to Hathor, by the personnel of the expeditions. The vast majority were written in Egyptian, but some of the monuments bore texts in a script (there were eleven such texts in all) that contained 'a mixture of Egyptian hieroglyphs . . . though not a word of regular Egyptian could be read'. One of these, a sphinx-statuette, is particularly interesting in that it bears   42
texts written both in ordinary Egyptian script and in the Sinaitic script. The Egyptian is inscribed between the paws and on the right shoulder, where it reads 'beloved of Hathor,

42 Sandstone sphinx statuette with inscriptions
  in Egyptian hieroglyphs and in Protosinaitic.
  Second Intermediate Period. Serabit
  el-Khadim. L. 23.7 cm. BM 41748.

58

43 Sphinx statuette, detail. Part of the Protosinaitic
inscription on the left side including the group
identified as 'Balat'.

mistress of turquoise', the Sinaitic is written on
both the right and left sides on the upper
surfaces of the pedestal. Petrie was unable to
offer any suggestions as to the reading of the
script but he did make some perceptive obser-
vations. He noted, for example, that in view of
the limited number of signs the new script was
likely to be alphabetic and that in view of the
context it probably represented the Semitic
language of the Asiatic workers on the staff of
the expeditions. Petrie dated the material to
the middle of the Eighteenth Dynasty but in
this he was probably wrong. The sculptural
style of the sphinx and of some of the other
pieces indicates an earlier date, in all likelihood
the late Middle Kingdom or Second Intermediate Period.

Table 2   The Sinaitic script appears to consist of at
least twenty-three separate signs, the forms of nearly half of which are clearly borrowed
from Egyptian. Like the hieroglyphs the signs are arranged either in columns or in
horizontal lines but they seem generally to read from left to right. There appears to have
been no strict rule as to which direction the individual signs should face, though within a
single text the direction is consistent. The first breakthrough in deciphering the system
was made in 1916 by the English scholar, A. H. (later Sir Alan) Gardiner (1879–1963).
He noticed that a number of the signs depicted objects or things, the Semitic names for
which correspond to the names of letters in the later Phoenician/Canaanite alphabet.
Gardiner was led to the conclusion that the linear forms of the latter were actually
derived from the Sinaitic 'pictograms' and showed that the transition in form from one
to the other was in many cases traceable without undue difficulty. Moreover in assigning
to the Sinai pictograms the phonetic values of their alphabetic descendants he was able

43   to read the commonly occurring group   as *bʿlt*, 'Balat'. This makes very good sense
in the context, since Balat is the name of a Semitic goddess closely identified with
Hathor, whose name, in addition, occurs written in Egyptian hieroglyphs, on the sphinx
that is one of the monuments bearing the group in question. Gardiner was unable to
make further progress with the material at hand, but the fact that by a process of logical
deduction, unforced by prejudice, the Sinai texts had been made to yield perhaps the one
name most likely to occur in the area has been regarded as a powerful factor in favour of
his interpretation of the script.

Since Gardiner's initial contribution, a great deal of scholarly work has been carried
out on Protosinaitic. The stock of available texts has more than trebled and these now
include inscriptions from places other than Sinai. Unfortunately the texts are invariably
short and often crudely executed. Progress in further understanding has been slow, and
has been limited on the whole to small gains in vocabulary. A complete decipherment of
the script published in 1966 by the American scholar W. F. Albright (1891–1971) has

Table 2: Protosinaitic signs and Egyptian prototypes (Protosinaitic forms after Albright).

not received general acceptance. Probably the most important development has been the realisation that the Sinaitic texts are not an isolated group. Inscriptions written in what appear to be basically the same script have been identified in various localities in Palestine. Some are roughly contemporary with the Sinaitic texts, others are later. The corpus as a whole, including the Sinai material, is now referred to by some scholars as Proto-Canaanite.

That the system represents an early stage in the history of the alphabet seems very feasible. Recent studies in the palaeography of the texts have tended to confirm its suggested relationship with the later Canaanite or Phoenician alphabet, though a link is not demonstrable in the case of every individual sign. The system is not strictly 'alphabetic' in the proper sense but is really an 'economical syllabary' in which each sign stands for a consonant + any vowel. In its creation the Egyptian writing system is thought to have been influential, supplying not only the actual sign-forms, or at least some of them, but also providing with its unisonsonantal signs a partial model for just such a restricted signary. If this view is correct (and it is not accepted by all scholars), it has an interesting implication. Since the Canaanite/Phoenician syllabary formed the basis of the Greek alphabet, and the Greek in turn of the Latin, it means, in the words of Gardiner, that 'the hieroglyphs live on, though in transmuted form, within our own alphabet'.

Table 3

Egyptian	Protosinaitic	Phoenician	Early Greek	Greek	Latin
				A	A
				B	B
				Γ	G
				E	E
				k	K
				M	M
				N	N
		o	o	O	O
				P	R
		×	T	T	T
		w		Σ	S

Table 3: From hieroglyphic sign to alphabetic letter.

Meroïtic

Meroïtic was the native language of a great African civilisation, known to the Egyptians as the 'Kingdom of Kush', which during the later periods of Egyptian history had its capital at Meroë (modern Begrawiya in the Sudan).

The language was first recorded in writing in the second century BC in an 'alphabetic' script consisting of twenty-three symbols, most of which were borrowed or at least derived from Egyptian writing. The system is quite different from Egyptian. Every sign has a phonetic value, and vowels as well as consonants are represented. There is also a special symbol for marking the division between words. The script has two forms, hieroglyphic and cursive. Hieroglyphic inscriptions are normally written in columns, cursive in horizontal lines reading from right to left. Unlike Egyptian the individual signs read in the direction which the figures face.

Although it looks alphabetic, Meroïtic is in fact a syllabic system. A 'consonantal' sign does not represent a single consonant but a consonant plus the vowel a, except when it is followed by one of the signs i, o and e. The special sign for the vowel a is used only at the beginning of words. There are separate signs for the combinations n + e, s + e, t + e, and t + o. In addition the sign for e has two uses: not only does it represent the vowel e, but it can also denote the lack of a vowel following a consonant.

The corpus of known Meroïtic inscriptions is much larger than that of Protosinaitic but is still relatively small. To date fewer than 1,000 individual texts have been properly

Table 4

Hieroglyphic	Cursive	Value	Hieroglyphic	Cursive	Value
		a			l
		e			ḫ
		i			ẖ
		o			š (s)
		y			se
		w			k
		b			q
		p			t
		m			te
		n			to
		ne			d
		r			word divider

Table 4: Meroïtic syllabary (after Hintze).

documented, though this total is increasing steadily. They have been found throughout the length of the Sudanese and Nubian Nile valley from Philae in the north to Naqa near Khartoum in the south and occur in a wide range of contexts – on temple walls, shrines, altars, offering tables, stelae, statues, pottery vessels, ostraca, papyri, and in the form of rock-graffiti. Inscriptions in the hieroglyphic script are comparatively rare and are largely confined to royal and divine 'prestige' contexts. Cursive is much more common. It was the 'everyday' script and gradually supplanted its ornamental companion. The earliest dated text in Meroïtic is a hieroglyphic temple inscription of Queen Shanakdakhete (c. 180–170 BC). There is no evidence for its use, in either form, after the fifth century AD.

The fundamental work on Meroïtic was carried out by the British Egyptologist, Francis Llewellyn Griffith (1862–1934), in the first decade or so of this century. By a detailed comparison of parallel funerary formulae occurring on offering tables and stelae, Griffith was able to determine the size of the Meroïtic syllabary, to prove the correlation between the hieroglyphic and cursive scripts, and to show in which direction the signs were to be read. He then went on to establish the phonetic values of the signs.

44 The key to this achievement was an inscription carved on the base of a sacred boat from the temple of Ban Naqa in the Sudan, now in the Berlin Museum. Included in this inscription are the cartouches of two rulers of Meroë, a king and a queen, Natakemeni and Amanitere, who were dedicators of the monument. The vital point is that the names are written in both Meroïtic and Egyptian hieroglyphs. Since the phonetic values of the Egyptian signs were known, it was possible for Griffith to deduce the values of the Meroïtic equivalents. The values of eight separate signs, over one third of the complete syllabary, were thus more or less correctly established from this one inscription. By cleverly isolating in other Meroïtic texts various well-known names such as those of the gods Osiris and Isis and place names like Philae, Griffith quickly established the values of the remaining signs. The system established by Griffith has since been refined and modified in points of detail, most notably by the German scholar Fritz Hintze, but it is agreed to have been essentially correct.

This success in transliterating the scripts has not, unfortunately, been followed by an equivalent progress in understanding the language which they write. Some words and phrases have been made out with reasonable certainty and some grammatical constructions tentatively identified, but the meaning of the vast majority of inscriptions remains obscure. The task of deciphering the language would be considerably aided if a link between Meroïtic and some other known language could be established. This has yet to be achieved. Meroïtic does not apparently belong to the Afro-Asiatic family and attempts to place it within one of the African groups of languages have hitherto proved inconclusive. It seems likely that really significant progress will have to await the discovery of a bilingual text, another 'Rosetta Stone', written in Meroïtic and some other known language, like Egyptian or Greek.

44 Stand from Ban Naga with inscriptions in Egyptian and Meroïtic hieroglyphs. 0-AD 20. H. 1.18 m. East Berlin, 7261.

Bibliography

Albright, William Foxwell, *The Proto-Sinaitic Inscriptions and their Decipherment*, Harvard/London, 1966

Andrews, Carol, *The Rosetta Stone*, London, 1981

Assmann, Aleida and Jan, and Christof Hardmeier (eds), *Schrift und Gedächtnis. Beiträge zur Archäologie der literarischen Kommunikation*, Munich, 1983

Baines, John, 'Literacy and Ancient Egyptian Society', *Man* 18, 1983, pp. 572–99

Baines, John R., 'Schreiben' in Wolfgang Helck and Wolfhart Westendorf (eds), *Lexikon der Ägyptologie*, V, Wiesbaden, 1984, cols 693–8

Bynon, James and Theodora (eds), *Hamito-Semitica. Proceedings of a Colloquium held by the Historical Section of the Linguistics Association (Great Britain) at the School of Oriental and African Studies, University of London, on the 18th, 19th and 20th of March 1970*, The Hague, 1975

Callender, John B., *Middle Egyptian*, Malibu, 1975

Caminos, Ricardo, and Henry G. Fischer, *Ancient Egyptian Epigraphy and Palaeography*, New York, 1976

Černý, J., *Paper and books in ancient Egypt*, London, 1952

Davies, Nina M., *Picture Writing in Ancient Egypt*, Oxford, 1958

Faulkner, Raymond O., *A Concise Dictionary of Middle Egyptian*, Oxford, 1962

Fischer, Henry George, *L'écriture et l'art de l'Égypte ancienne. Quatre leçons sur la paléographie et l'épigraphie pharaoniques*, Paris, 1986

Fischer, Henry George, *Egyptian Studies*, II. *The Orientation of Hieroglyphs*, Part 1 *Reversals*, New York, 1977

Fischer, Henry G., 'Hieroglyphen' in Wolfgang Helck and Wolfhart Westendorf (eds), *Lexikon der Ägyptologie*, II, Wiesbaden, 1977, cols 1189–99

Galeries nationales du Grand Palais, *Naissance de l'écriture. Cuneiformes et hiéroglyphes*, exh. cat., Paris, 1982

Gardiner, Alan H., 'The Egyptian Origin of the Semitic Alphabet', *The Journal of Egyptian Archaeology* 3, 1916, pp. 1–16

Gardiner, Sir Alan, *Egyptian Grammar. Being an Introduction to the Study of Hieroglyphs*, 3rd edn (rev.), Oxford, 1957

Gaur, Albertine, *A History of Writing*, London, 1984

Gelb, I. J., *A Study of Writing. A discussion of the general principles governing the use and evolution of writing*, rev. edn, Chicago, 1963

Griffith, F. L., *Meroitic Inscriptions*, Parts I and II, London, 1911 and 1912

Harris, J. R. (ed.), *The Legacy of Egypt*, 2nd edn, Oxford, 1971

Harris, Roy, *The Origin of Writing*, London, 1986

Hawkins, J. D., 'The origin and dissemination of writing in western Asia' in P. R. S. Moorey (ed.), *The Origins of Civilization*, Oxford, 1979, pp. 128–66

Henderson, Leslie, *Orthography and Word Recognition in Reading*, London, 1982

Hintze, Fritz, 'The Meroitic Period' in *Africa in Antiquity. The Arts of Ancient Nubia and the Sudan* I. *The Essays*, Brooklyn Museum exh. cat., Brooklyn, 1978, pp. 89–105

Hodge, Carleton T. (ed.), *Afroasiatic. A Survey*, The Hague, 1971

Iversen, Erik, *The Myth of Egypt and its Hieroglyphs in European Tradition*, Copenhagen, 1961

Lewis, Naphtali, *Papyrus in Classical Antiquity*, Oxford, 1974

Lichtheim, M., *Ancient Egyptian Literature*, 3 vols, California, 1973–80

Meltzer, E. S., 'Remarks on ancient Egyptian writing with emphasis on its mnemonic aspects' in Paul A. Kolers, Merald E. Wrolstad and Herman Bouma (eds), *Processing of Visible Language* 2, New York/London, 1980

Millard, A. R., 'The Infancy of the Alphabet', *World Archaeology*, 17, no. 3, 1986, pp. 390–8

Pope, Maurice, *The Story of Decipherment from Egyptian hieroglyphic to Linear B*, London, 1975

Quaegebeur, J., 'De la préhistoire de l'écriture Copte', *Orientalia Lovaniensia Periodica* 13, Leuven, 1982, pp. 125–36

Ray, John D., 'The Emergence of Writing in Egypt', *World Archaeology* 17, no. 3, 1986, pp. 307–16

Sampson, Geoffrey, *Writing Systems. A linguistic introduction*, London, 1985

Schäfer, Heinrich, *Principles of Egyptian Art*, ed., with an epilogue, by Emma Brunner-Traut; trans. and ed., with an introduction, by John Baines, Oxford, 1974

Shinnie, P. L., *Meroe: a civilization of the Sudan*, London, 1967

Schenkel, Wolfgang, 'Schrift' in Wolfgang Helck and Wolfhart Westendorf (eds), *Lexikon der Ägyptologie*, V, Wiesbaden, 1984, cols 713–35

Schenkel, Wolfgang, 'The structure of hieroglyphic script', *Royal Anthropological Institute News*, 15, 1976, pp. 4–7

Williams, R. J., 'Scribal training in ancient Egypt', *Journal of the American Oriental Society* 92, 1972, pp. 214–21

Index

DATE DUE

NOV 04 9			

...CAN-
AMERICAN
COLLECTIVE
BIOGRAPHIES

Celebrated African-American Novelists

Amy Graham

Enslow Publishers, Inc.
40 Industrial Road
Box 398
Berkeley Heights, NJ 07922
USA
http://www.enslow.com

Library of Congress Cataloging-in-Publication Data:

Graham, Amy.
    Celebrated African-American novelists / by Amy Graham.
        p. cm. — (African-American collective biographies)
    Summary: "Read about important African American novelists including: Harriet
      Adams Wilson, Zora Neale Hurston, Richard Wright, Ralph Ellison, James Baldwin,
      Alex Haley, Toni Morrison, Ernest Gaines, and Alice Walker"—Provided by publisher.
    Includes bibliographical references and index.
    ISBN 978-1-59845-138-2
    1. African American novelists—Biography—Juvenile literature. 2. Novelists, Ameri-
    can—20th century—Biography—Juvenile literature. I. Title.
    PS153.N5G684 2012
    813.009'896073—dc23

                                   2011019953

Future editions:
Paperback ISBN 978-1-4644-0037-7
ePUB ISBN 978-1-4645-0944-5
PDF ISBN 978-1-4646-0944-2

Printed in the United States of America

032012 Lake Book Manufacturing, Inc., Melrose Park, IL

10 9 8 7 6 5 4 3 2 1

To Our Readers: We have done our best to make sure all Internet addresses in this book
were active and appropriate when we went to press. However, the author and the publisher have no control over and assume no liability for the material available on those
Internet sites or on other Web sites they may link to. Any comments or suggestions can
be sent by e-mail to comments@enslow.com or to the address on the back cover.

♻ Enslow Publishers, Inc., is committed to printing our books on recycled paper. The
paper in every book contains 10% to 30% post-consumer waste (PCW). The cover board
on the outside of each book contains 100% PCW. Our goal is to do our part to help young
people and the environment too!

Illustration Credits: AP Images, pp. 7, 40, 44, 52, 58, 73, 78; AP Images: David Book-
staver, p. 70, John Amis, p. 88, Laura Sikes, p. 92, Nancy Kaye, p. 48, Thibault Camus,
p. 67; Everett Collection, p. 83; Library of Congress, pp. 6, 20, 24, 30, 34; National Ar-
chives and Records Administration, pp. 5, 8, 14; Tina Perrotta, p. 10; U. S. Coast Guard,
p. 62.

Cover Illustration: AP Images/Thibault Camus

Contents

Introduction

This book describes the lives of some of the most important African-American writers of novels. A novel is a work of fiction. It is a story created from the imagination of the author. Each author in this book descended from people brought to the United States from Africa to work as slaves. Slaves rarely had the chance to learn to read or write. It was largely not until after the end of slavery in the United States that African Americans began to write novels. With *Our Nig* (1859), Harriet Wilson became the first African American to publish a novel in the United States. Wilson was a free black woman who lived in New Hampshire. While working as a domestic servant, she received a basic education. Unlike southern slave states, northern states such as New Hampshire did not prohibit African Americans from learning to read and write.

After the Civil War, the United States passed the Thirteenth Amendment to the Constitution to abolish slavery and extend full citizenship to newly freed African Americans. But conditions were slow to improve, especially in the South. African Americans struggled to exercise basic civil rights. States enacted Jim Crow laws, which made it difficult for blacks to vote, enter whites-only restaurants, sit at the front of a bus, or even borrow books from a public library. Lynchings took place. These problems, and economic exploitation, led many African Americans to flee the South for northern cities such as Chicago, Detroit, and New York, where they often found better living conditions. But for some, life in city slums was just a different kind of misery.

Black culture grew stronger in New York in the 1920s. Harlem was a place rich in creativity. Jazz music flourished. African-American writers gained financial support through grants, stipends, and the Federal Writers' Project. Zora Neale Hurston wrote about black folklore, capturing the colorful language and stories of her Florida childhood. Later, Richard Wright wrote his novel *Native Son*. It shocked the nation with its grim portrayal of the African-American experience.

Race relations remained poor in the South. In this context, Ralph Ellison wrote his classic novel *Invisible Man*. It highlighted

A line of chained slaves being transported to market was a common sight in cities throughout the South.

A view of Seventh Avenue in Harlem, New York City, during the Harlem Renaissance

how unfair life was for many African Americans. Writers Richard Wright and James Baldwin fled overseas to France, where they felt more accepted. But times were changing. Jackie Robinson broke baseball's color barrier. *Brown v. Board of Education* deemed "separate but equal" schooling unconstitutional. In 1955, Rosa Parks's refusal to give up her seat on the bus began the Montgomery Bus Boycott, which ran 381 days before the U.S. Supreme Court declared Alabama's bus segregation laws unconstitutional.

With the *Brown* v. *Board of Education* decision requiring integration in schools, the civil rights movement began.

Rev. Martin Luther King Jr. led peaceful protests for civil rights throughout the South during the 1950s and 60s.

Introduction

During the 1950s and 1960s Rev. Martin Luther King, Jr. led peaceful protests for civil rights throughout the South. At the same time, in northern cities, Malcolm X and other militants preached that change could only come about through violent revolution. Author Alex Haley helped Malcolm X write the story of his life. But with the assassinations of Malcolm X and Dr. King, it seemed that times could not change fast enough. In the 1970s writers such as Toni Morrison and Alice Walker described the experiences of African-American women. Their powerful novels helped the nation heal from the deep wounds of slavery. Author Ernest Gaines was born in the Deep South. He broke the popular mold of novels about black urban life. Gaines writes compellingly about the black experience in the rural South.

Novels are works of imaginative art that represent their author's ideas and attitudes. When a book reaches a wide audience, it introduces society to new ideas. In this way, novels can bring about change. The works of the writers in this book have helped promote understanding of the black experience in America.

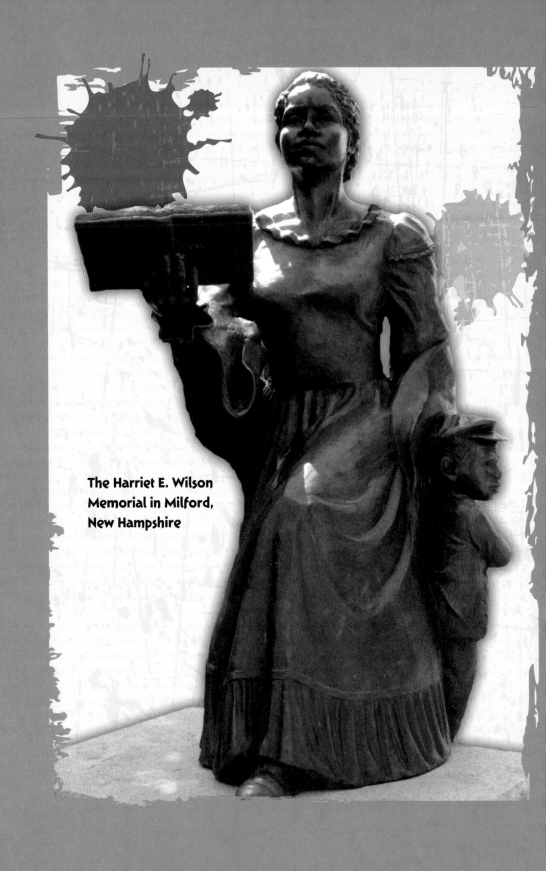

The Harriet E. Wilson
Memorial in Milford,
New Hampshire

Chapter 1

Harriet Adams Wilson

It was rare for enslaved African Americans to have the opportunity to learn to read or write. It is not surprising, then, that the first African-American novelist was not a slave. Harriet Wilson was a free woman living in the North. She was thirty-four years old when she published her book in 1859. In the fashion of the day, the title was long and descriptive: *Our Nig: Sketches from the Life of a Free Black, in a Two-Story White House, North: Showing that Slavery's Shadow Falls Even There.* Her novel is about an abandoned black girl who must work as a servant for a white family. The mother of the family cruelly abuses the girl, who longs to be loved and respected. Though it was a work of fiction, Wilson based much of her novel on events from her life.[1]

Life in the Free North

Wilson was born Harriet E. Adams on March 15, 1825, in Milford, New Hampshire. Her mother, Margaret Smith, was white. Her father, Joshua Green, was a free African American. It was forty years before the downfall of slavery in America. Thus, as she says in the title of her book, Wilson was a free black woman. At the time of Harriet's birth, many African Americans worked on plantations in the South as slaves. In New England, it was against the law to own slaves. Some New Englanders opposed slavery for moral reasons. Ministers preached on Sundays about its evils, and newspapers printed articles condemning it. People who spoke out against slavery were called abolitionists. They worked to abolish, or end, slavery. The call for abolition was one of the causes of the U.S. Civil War. It helped bring about the end of slavery with the passage of the Thirteenth Amendment. But what was life like for a young African-American girl growing up in the free North?

Deserted by Kindred

Harriet Wilson's father died when she was very young. After his death, Harriet's mother abandoned her. She left her on the doorstep of a farm owned by the well-to-do Nehemiah Hayward Jr. He and his family decided to take the little girl in. Harriet was just six years old when she became a servant at the Hayward farm. Indentured servitude was common in the early days of America. For many, it was a way for a person to work off a debt. Poor immigrants sometimes paid the cost of their trip across the Atlantic by becoming indentured servants. They did not earn money. They worked in hopes of earning their freedom. Children like Harriet who were orphaned or abandoned had no choice in the matter.

In her novel, a mulatto girl (based on Wilson) is treated poorly by her adoptive family. Because of the color of her father's skin, they treat her as a second-class citizen. They beat her and call her names. It can only be assumed that the girl's treatment mirrors Wilson's experiences.

It is known, however, that she blamed her years at the Hayward farm for her ill health as a young woman.

Free at Last

When Harriet was eighteen, she was finally free to leave the Hayward farm. She was trained as a house servant, but she had also had some schooling. With the help of friends, she learned to weave straw hats. She became active in the movement to abolish slavery. That was how she met her husband, Thomas Wilson. A lecturer on the abolition circuit, he was a fugitive slave, or so he said. Wilson and Thomas were married in October 1851. They had a baby boy, George Mason Wilson, in the spring of 1852. But not long afterward Thomas left his wife and son. It turned out he had lied about who he was: He had not been a slave after all.

Wilson was left alone once again, and now with a baby to support. She was too sick to work. Brokenhearted, she realized she had no choice but to put her young son in foster care. She wanted desperately to earn enough money to take care of him. She turned to writing as a way to make money. Many people in the North were interested in abolition. Perhaps people would buy a book that told her story, that of a free black treated no better than a slave. A Boston publisher agreed to print her book.

In the preface of *Our Nig*, Wilson pleads with readers to purchase the book. She explains that it is the only means she has to support her child. The book ends with letters of testimony by white people who vouch for her honesty and integrity. They encourage readers to buy the book to support its author. Tragically, within five months after Wilson's book came out, her son fell sick with a terrible fever. He died in 1860 at the age of seven.

13

A group of slaves on a plantation in 1864. Slavery was a brutal institution. Harriet Wilson became active in the movement to abolish it.

In time, Wilson regained her health. She found new ways to earn a living. These included palmistry (palm-reading), nursing, and traveling around New England as a hair-dye peddler. Copies of *Our Nig* have been found along her sales route. She peddled her book, along with her tonics, when she found a sympathetic audience.[2]

Painful Truth is Hard to Face

Uncle Tom's Cabin, a novel about slavery in the South by Harriet Beecher Stowe, was a bestseller in 1852. It sold ten thousand copies within a week and three hundred thousand within a year.[3] *Our Nig* never met with this kind of success. It was not even reviewed in Boston newspapers. Why? Like Stowe's book it brought up some very uncomfortable questions. Was making a child work as a servant any different from owning a slave? The abolitionists spoke passionately about ending slavery. Yet even in the North black people did not have equal rights. Wilson's story may have hit too close for comfort. That may be why it was not widely read in abolitionist circles.[4]

A Turn to the Spiritual

Later in life, Wilson moved to the Boston area. She was listed as a "trance reader and lecturer" in *Banner of Light*, a Spiritualist newspaper, from 1870 until 1897.[5] Spiritualists believe that it is possible to communicate with spirits. They hold candlelit meetings called séances. In a séance a medium, or person said to have the power to speak with spirits, falls into a deeply relaxed state. While under the trance, the medium becomes a channel for spirits to speak through. Séances were a popular pastime in the late 1800s. People who attended found it a comfort to "hear from" deceased loved ones. Wilson also strove to improve work conditions for children. A marriage certificate shows that on September 29, 1870, she married, albeit briefly, for a second time. Her husband was John Gallatin Robinson, a white Spiritualist. Census information indicates that the couple did not stay together.[6]

15

Wilson died on June 28, 1900, at the age of seventy-five. For years her name went unknown and unspoken. That changed in the early 1980s thanks to Professor Henry Louis Gates Jr. of Harvard University. Gates was researching early African-American literature when he

found Wilson's son's death certificate. This proved that the author of *Our Nig* was African-American. People had believed that the little-known book was written by a white abolitionist. Scholars had previously thought Frances E. W. Harper was the first African American to publish a novel.[7] Her book *Iola Leroy* came out in 1892, more than thirty years after *Our Nig*.

Remembering Wilson

The Harriet Wilson Project works to spread the word about Harriet Wilson and her role in American literature. The group continues to search for more clues about Wilson's life. In 2006, it erected a memorial statue in Milford, New Hampshire. The statue portrays a graceful, young black woman. She stands tall and proud. In her hands she holds a book. The young boy standing with her is her son, George Mason Wilson.

Harriet Adams Wilson Timeline

1825—Harriet E. Adams is born on March 15 in Milford, New Hampshire.

1830–1831—Adams is abandoned by her mother at Nehemiah Hayward's family farm.

1840—Adams is listed as a 22-year-old living with Boyle family on the federal census for Milford, New Hampshire.

1851—Adams marries Thomas Wilson on October 6 in Milford, New Hampshire.

1852—Harriet E. Wilson gives birth to son George Mason Wilson in May or June.

1855–1859—Wilson and/or her son appears in the "Report of the Overseers of the Poor" for the town of Milford, New Hampshire.

1859—Wilson copyrights *Our Nig* on August 18; a copy of the novel is deposited in the Office of the Clerk of the U.S. District Court of Massachusetts.

1859—*Our Nig* is published on September 5.

1860—George Mason Wilson, Harriet Wilson's son, dies in Milford at the Poor farm, age seven years, eight months on September 16.

1863—Wilson appears on the "Report of the Overseers of the Poor" for the town of Milford.

1867—Wilson is listed in the Boston Spiritualist newspaper *Banner of Light* as living in East Cambridge, Massachusetts. She is known in Spiritualist circles as "the colored medium."

1870—Wilson is married to John Gallatin Robinson in Boston on September 29.

1870–1897—"Mrs. Hattie E. Wilson" is listed in the *Banner of Light* as a trance reader and lecturer.

1900—Wilson dies on June 28 in Quincy Hospital, Massachusetts.

1982—Wilson's novel *Our Nig* is rediscovered by Henry Louis Gates Jr.

Zora Neale Hurston

Zora Neale Hurston is the best-known female writer of the Harlem Renaissance. Her novel *Their Eyes Were Watching God* is taught in schools across the country. She published four novels, two collections of folktales, and an autobiography. She also wrote more than a hundred short stories, several plays, and many essays and articles.

Childhood in Eatonville, Florida

Hurston was born on January 7, 1891, in the town of Notasulga in Macon County, Alabama. She was the fifth of eight children. Her parents, John and Lucy Potts Hurston, did not want to pick cotton in the fields as their enslaved parents had. John Hurston supported the family as a tenant farmer and carpenter; Lucy worked occasionally as a schoolteacher. The family moved to Eatonville, Florida, when Zora was three. White settlers of the nearby town of Maitland paid well for help clearing land and building homes. Established in 1882, Eatonville was the first incorporated African-American community in the United States. Every resident was black, from the

19

Zora Neale Hurston's most famous novel is *Their Eyes Were Watching God.*

mayor to the storekeeper. Growing up in an all-black town seems to have been instrumental to Hurston. Having strong role models gave her the confidence to follow her dreams.[1]

"Jump at de sun"

In addition to his other jobs, John Hurston was a Baptist minister who also served three terms as mayor. He expected his eight children to be well-behaved. Zora, spirited and sassy, worried her father, who thought she was too outspoken for her own good. In the American South at the turn of the century, African Americans lived in fear of lynching and other brutal violence. Zora's father lectured to her that she would come to no good if she did not learn her place. Her mother understood her better and often stuck up for her. She did not want to "squinch" her daughter's spirit and have her turn into a "mealy-mouthed rag doll."[2] Hurston remembered her mother encouraging her children to "'jump at de sun.' We might not land on the sun, but at least we would get off the ground," Hurston wrote in her autobiography, *Dust Tracks on a Road.*

By her own account, Hurston was a curious child who loved adventure. Her mother wondered if someone hadn't spread "travel dust" on the doorstep the day she was born.[3] Hurston remembered as a young girl sitting on the gatepost in her front yard, looking out over the road that led to Orlando. As carriages went by, she called out, "Don't you want me to go a piece of the way with you?" Quite often, the white people going by were charmed by her and accepted her offer. She would ride and chat with them a bit before they let her down to run home. These antics earned her a whipping and concerned her grandmother, a former slave, to no end. She worried

21

what trouble her young granddaughter might fall into.[4] Confronted with a world where people wanted her to be something less than what she was, Hurston withdrew into her imagination.

End of Childhood

When Zora was thirteen, her childhood came crashing to an end when her mother, who had long been ill, passed away. To make matters worse, her father remarried within six months. His new wife was just twenty years old and wanted nothing to do with her new stepchildren. Zora was sent to boarding school. When the end of the school year arrived, her father sent word that the school could adopt her. Brokenhearted, Zora went to live with her older siblings, who had homes of their own. She bounced around from house to house and spent her time feeling miserable. She worked for a time as a maid and a nanny, but she wished she could go to school. Her luck changed when she took a job assisting a woman who sang in a Gilbert and Sullivan traveling show. There she met a group of educated people with a love of books and the arts. She traveled around the Southeast. The experience opened her eyes to life's possibilities.

In 1917, Hurston decided to get her high school diploma. There was just one problem: At twenty-six, she was too old to attend. She solved this by shaving ten years off her life, claiming she was born January 7, 1901. She kept this birthdate for the rest of her life.[5]

Most students at Morgan Academy (now Morgan State University) came from upper-middle-class families. Hurston was poor. She wore the same dress to school each day. Still, with her bright personality and quick wit, she made friends easily. Whenever there was a dance, her friends would loan her a dress.[6]

Hurston did well in school. English was her favorite subject. Her friends encouraged her to go on to college. She applied to Howard University in Washington, D.C. It was the most prestigious school for African Americans in the nation. At Howard, she published her first short story in the college literary magazine, *The Stylus*. She received an associate's degree from Howard University in 1920.

A Fresh Voice of the Harlem Renaissance

Charles Johnson, founder of *Opportunity: A Journal of Negro Life*, saw Hurston's story in *The Stylus*. He encouraged her to write more. He suggested she come to New York City. There were many African-American writers and artists living in Harlem. Hurston moved there in 1925 and enrolled at Barnard College to study English. She also took classes with Columbia University's famous anthropologist Franz Boas. Her stories began to appear regularly in *Opportunity*. She entered an *Opportunity* literary contest. Both her play and her short story won second prize.

As a writer, Hurston had a talent for dialect. She was able to capture on the page how people spoke, from their accents to their choice of words and phrases. These details bring her characters to life. Hurston always claimed that she learned her love of stories as a girl on the front porch of Joe Clarke's general store. The men sat on boxes in the shade in the heat of the day. They gossiped and told tall tales. Little girls were not supposed to listen in, but Hurston found a way to linger whenever she could.[7]

23

A Published Writer and World Traveler

In 1928, Hurston graduated from Barnard with a bachelor's degree in English. She was the school's first African-American graduate. Her mentor, Franz Boas,

When Hurston (far left) was a child, her mother told her to "Jump at de sun." In later years, she still liked to play and have fun.

arranged for her to travel to Florida to collect folktales. She also received funding from a patron of the arts named Charlotte O. Mason. Mason, a wealthy white society woman, insisted Hurston call her "Godmother." Mason had an interest in what she called "nativism": African-American and Native American folk culture.

From 1927 through 1932, Mason gave Hurston funds to travel and collect folktales. Hurston returned to the South to collect stories. She studied magic voodoo ceremonies in New Orleans. She went to the Bahamas, where she survived a five-day hurricane. In 1932 she returned to Eatonville to pull together her notes for a book. One of her short stories, "The Gilded Six-Bit," appeared in *Story* magazine. A publisher approached Hurston. Did she have a novel? Hurston replied that she did, and then set off to work on one. Her novel, *Jonah's Gourd Vine*, came out in 1934. It was the story of a preacher, John, and his long-suffering wife, Lucy. A review in the *New York Times* hailed it as "the most vital and original novel about the American Negro that has yet been written by a member of the Negro race." Her book of folklore, *Mules and Men*, followed in 1935.

In 1936 Hurston was awarded a grant from the Guggenheim Foundation. With these funds, she visited the Caribbean islands of Jamaica and Haiti. There she learned about the voodoo religion and folklore of the descendants of Africans. Her book on the subject, *Tell My Horse: Voodoo and Life in Haiti and Jamaica*, came out in 1938.

While in Haiti, Hurston was inspired to write a second novel. She completed *Their Eyes Were Watching God* in just seven weeks. It tells the story of Janie Crawford, an independent young black woman. Today it is considered a classic of American literature, but critics of the day were not so sure. With its unapologetic, strong female lead and proud black southern dialogue, the book was very different from what they were used to reading.

A Writer in Her Prime

Hurston's third novel, *Moses, Man of the Mountain*, came out in 1939. It explores the biblical story of Moses. Her publisher now encouraged her to work on her autobiography. Hurston reluctantly agreed. She found it hard to write. To her frustration, the publisher heavily censored her political views. But when *Dust Tracks on a Road* came out in 1942, it sold well. The book won the *Saturday Review's* Anisfield-Wolf Book Award in race relations. Black critics were disappointed. They contended that she had written the book for a white audience.[8]

In 1947 Hurston traveled by boat to Honduras, where she planned to search for the ruins of a lost Mayan city. She spent her time there completing her novel *Seraph on the Suwanee*. Published the following year, the book was about the marriage of a white couple in rural Florida. It sold well, but critics wondered why Hurston had turned her back on her source of inspiration, black folklore.[9] She worked on several more novels but could not find a publisher.

Struggling to Make Ends Meet

In need of money, Hurston took a job in 1950 as a maid for a white family, until someone recognized her. The *Miami Herald* ran an article entitled "Famous Negro Author Working as Maid Here Just to Live a Little." She later found work in a library and writing articles for newspapers. All of her books had gone out of print. When Hurston suffered a stroke in 1959, she was left in poverty. Unable to care for herself and too proud to contact her family, she went to live in the St. Lucie County Welfare Home. She died of heart disease on January 28, 1960. Her friends took up a collection to pay for the funeral, but there was not enough for a gravestone.

26

Walker Pays Homage

Writer Alice Walker felt a sense of homecoming when she first read Hurston's work. "Reading her, I saw for the first time my own specific culture.... I felt as if, indeed,

I had been given a map that led to the remains of my literary country."[10] Pretending to be Hurston's niece, she made a pilgrimage to Florida in 1973 to find Hurston's grave. Wading through deep grass, she located the spot and had a gravestone placed there. It reads "Zora Neale Hurston, A Genius of the South: Novelist, Folklorist, Anthropologist."

Zora Neale Hurston Timeline

1891— Zora Neale Hurston is born on January 7 in Notasulga, Alabama. She will move to Eatonville, Florida as a toddler.

1904— Lucy Potts Hurston (mother) dies, and her father quickly remarries.

1917—Hurston takes 10 years off her age (to present herself as 16) and goes back to finish high school.

1925—Hurston moves to Harlem and goes to Barnard College.

1928—Hurston graduates from Barnard College.

1937—*Their Eyes Were Watching God* is published.

1938—*Tell My Horse* is published.

1939—*Moses, Man of the Mountain* is published.

1942—*Dust Tracks on a Road* is published.

1948—*Seraph on the Suwanee* is published.

1960—Hurston dies on January 28 in Fort Pierce, Florida. She is buried on February 7 in an unmarked grave.

1973—Alice Walker has a headstone placed at Hurston's grave.

Chapter 3

Richard Wright

Born near Natchez, Mississippi, in 1908, Richard Wright grew up very poor. His illiterate father, Nathaniel Wright, tired of working in the cotton fields, moved his family to Memphis, Tennessee. But in Memphis he deserted his wife and two sons and refused to pay child support. Richard's mother, Ella Wilson Wright, had been a schoolteacher before she married, but few white-collar jobs were open to black women. She found work as a cook, but suffered from ill health and was at times too sick to work. Richard and his little brother Leon were always hungry. During the day, Richard could ignore his hunger, but it grew so painful that he would wake up at night.[1]

Unable to pay the rent and without enough money to buy train tickets back to Mississippi, the trio had no place to go. Ella sent her sons to live in an orphanage. Wright remembered it as crowded and noisy. The headmistress gave the children bread with molasses twice a day. Richard was so hungry he had dizzy spells and lost consciousness. He grew afraid that he would never see his mother again.[2] He ran away, only to be badly beaten when a

Richard Wright was an author and a poet.

police officer found him and sent him back. As soon as his mother could, she took the boys back to Mississippi with her to live with family. They moved frequently, staying with various aunts and uncles. The boys rarely went to school.

A Lesson in Fear

In 1918 Ella moved with the boys to Elaine, Arkansas, to live with her sister Maggie and Maggie's husband Silas. Uncle Silas owned a saloon where black millworkers would go for a drink after work. For the first time, Richard had plenty of food.[3] He ate until he was stuffed and hid biscuits in his pockets for later. Silas slept with a gun under his pillow. He had received death threats from white men. They resented his success and wanted him to leave town, or else.[4] One day Silas did not return home. A friend came to the house with the horrible news that Silas had been murdered. The women and boys quickly packed and fled the town to avoid further violence. Richard had heard tales of white men beating and killing black people. Now the stories had become all too real.

Living in Segregation

In 1919 Ella had a stroke that left her unable to walk. She and the boys returned to Mississippi to live with her mother, Margaret Bolden Wilson, a light-skinned, illiterate ex-slave. At the train station, Richard had seen that there were separate lines for black people and white people. He was confused. But when he asked his mother about it, she grew angry and hit him.[5]

Margaret Wilson discouraged Richard's interest in stories, which she said were the work of the devil. She sent him to Howe Institute, a Seventh Day Adventist school, but he chafed against the strict rules. He transferred to

31

the public school, where he excelled in his classes and made friends. In eighth grade he wrote his first short story, "The Voodoo of Hell's Half Acre." It was so good that the *Southern Register*, a local African-American paper, published it. Richard's family was not proud, however. They told him that a black boy should not write; it was sure to get him in trouble.[6]

Self-Educated

Richard graduated at the top of his junior high class, but dropped out of high school to support himself. He took a job as a porter at a clothing store, but he did not act as white people expected him to. He did not smile and laugh, and he was soon fired.[7] Richard began to dream of going north, where race relations were rumored to be better. He moved to Jackson, Mississippi, where he stayed for two years, living frugally and saving as much as he could. His one splurge was to buy magazines. He would read them very carefully and resell them. One day he read about a white author named H. L. Mencken who spoke out strongly against racism. Richard wanted to read Mencken's books. Blacks were not allowed to borrow books from the library, so he talked a white coworker into letting him take books out on his card. Reading works by Theodore Dreiser, Sherwood Anderson, and Sinclair Lewis, Richard was amazed by what he read. He saw that words could be used as a weapon to fight injustice.[8] He began to write in the evenings after work and dreamed of writing his own novel.

32

Escape to the Windy City

In 1927, at age seventeen, Richard boarded a train for Chicago. When he arrived, he was amazed to see white and black people sitting beside one another on the bus.[9]

He found jobs, including substitute letter-sorter at the U.S. Postal Service. The machines were loud, and sorting the mail was dull, but the pay was good. He hoped to get a full-time job there, but to do so he would need to pass a medical exam. Due to years of going hungry, he weighed less than the mandatory 125 pounds. His irregular work schedule enabled him to continue writing.

Wright made many friends at work. Chicago was a city full of immigrants. His coworkers came from all different backgrounds. They talked together about how all people should have basic human rights. Wright felt hopeful that the world could change. Some of his friends belonged to the American Communist Party. They encouraged Wright to join the John Reed Club, a Communist writers' group. The group's literary magazine, *Left Front*, published his poems.

Wright was careful not to bring his friends home. He lived in a crowded, squalid apartment on the south side of Chicago with his brother, mother, and two aunts. In his spare time, Wright was hard at work on a novel called *Lawd Today* about black workers in Chicago. It was the first book he wrote, but he never saw it in print. It was only published after his death.

Finding Success in New York

In 1937 Wright turned down a full-time job with the post office. He had decided to move to New York City to become a writer. He took a job as the Harlem editor of the *Daily Worker*, a Communist newspaper. Wright agreed with many of the Communist ideals. But the party leaders put pressure on him to write about politics.[10] This did not sit well with Wright. He had his own ideas about what he would write. He left the *Daily Worker* to work for the Federal Writers' Project (FWP), a relief program

Images of poverty in southern Mississippi seared into Wright's memories. Many farmers lived in tumble-down shacks like this sharecropper's cabin in Jackson.

34

that employed six thousand writers to "write up" local geographies and document the lives of ordinary people. Wright used his connection with the Illinois FWP to collect stories and prepare the first draft of *Native Son*.

In 1937 Wright entered four short stories into a national contest. He won first prize and attracted the attention of a publisher. The publisher released his stories under the title *Uncle Tom's Children*. Wright received a Guggenheim Fellowship. This allowed him to finish *Native Son*, which was published in 1940. It was widely acclaimed as a powerful story about racial issues in America. It became the Book-of-the-Month Club's first selection of a book by an African-American author. In 1941 Wright won the NAACP Spingarn Medal for the most notable achievement by a black American. By 1942 he had split completely from the Communist Party. But Wright had caught the attention of the Federal Bureau of Investigation, which kept a file on him and monitored his activities.[11]

In 1939 Wright married Dhimah Rhose Meadman, a white modern dancer, with Ralph Ellison as best man. But within months he filed for a divorce. It had been a mistake: They did not get along. In 1941 he remarried. His wife, Ellen Poplar, was a white woman and a fellow Communist. She was the daughter of Jewish immigrants from Poland. Like many people of the time, her parents did not like the idea of interracial marriage.[12] Wright and Poplar had married because they were in love. They did not care what other people thought. They had two daughters, Julia in 1942 and Rachel in 1949.

Native Son Moves to France

In 1946 the Wrights moved to Paris. They were fed up with attitudes in the United States, where people could not accept that people of different races could marry. On trips to France, the Wrights had felt welcomed and accepted.[13] Richard Wright became a French citizen in 1947. He made friends with French existentialist authors Albert Camus and Jean-Paul Sartre. Existentialism is a form of philosophy that centers on the importance of a person's choices. Wright's next novel, *The Outsider* (1953), reflected this focus. It received mixed reviews. *The Savage Holiday*, his only book to feature all white characters, came out the following year. It did not do well either.

The Long Dream was published in 1957. It told the story of a black family in Mississippi, but the book drew fire from critics. Critics saw Wright as no longer in touch with race issues in America.[14]

Fighting for Social Justice

Wright was interested in the plight of people around the world. In the 1950s, he traveled to Africa, Indonesia, and Spain. He wrote about the things he saw. On a trip to Africa he caught amoebic dysentery. This intestinal illness is caused by a parasite. While sick, Wright distracted himself by writing haiku, a form of Japanese poetry.[15] He completed more than four thousand poems. A collection entitled *Haiku: This Other World* was issued in 1998.

Legacy of the Native Son

On November 28, 1960, Wright died of a heart attack in Paris. He was fifty-two years old. Wright was buried in the Père Lachaise Cemetery in Paris. He had known extreme hunger, poverty, and cruelty as a boy growing up in the American South. As a result, Wright had a strong sense of social justice. Without formal schooling, he taught himself how to communicate his anger and frustration with his writing. His books, including the autobiography *Black Boy* (1945), told the story of racism in America and helped bring about change.

Richard Wright Timeline

1908—Richard Wright is born on September 4 in Mississippi.

1924—Wright's first short story, "The Voodoo of Hell's Half Acre" is published in the *Southern Register*.

1925—Wright graduates Smith Robertson Junior High School in Jackson as the class valedictorian in June.

1927—Wright moves to Chicago.

1933—Wright joins the John Reed Club.

1937—Wright moves to New York City and helps start *New Challenge* magazine.

1938—*Uncle Tom's Children*, a collection of short stories, is published.

1939— Wright marries Dhimah Rose Meadman.

1940—*Native Son* is published. It is the first Book-of-the-Month Club selection by an African-American writer. Wright and Meadman divorce.

1941—Wright is awarded the NAACP Spingarn Medal. He marries Ellen Poplar.

1945—*Black Boy* is published.

1947—Wright and his family move to Paris, France.

1953—*The Outsider* is published.

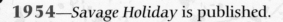

1954—*Savage Holiday* is published.

1960—Wright dies of a heart attack on November 28. He is buried at the Père Lachaise Cemetery in Paris.

1961—*Eight Men*, a collection of short stories, is published posthumously.

1963—*Lawd Today* is published posthumously.

1998—*Haiku: This Other World* is published posthumously.

Ralph Ellison

Ralph Ellison is the author of the classic novel *Invisible Man*. He won the National Book Award for the book in 1953. He was the first African American to win this important award. He also wrote two books of essays.

Growing Up in Oklahoma City

Ralph Waldo Ellison was born on March 1, 1914, and grew up in Oklahoma City. Oklahoma was still a young state, having gained statehood in 1907. Ralph's father, Lewis Ellison, had his own business selling ice and coal. At the time, people used blocks of ice to keep food from spoiling. Sometimes Lewis let his young son ride along on the cart while he delivered his wares. Sadly, one day three-year-old Ralph watched as his father slipped while lifting a heavy block of ice down into a dirt cellar. A shard of ice pierced his father's stomach. Lewis Ellison was rushed to the hospital in a horse-drawn ambulance, but it was too late. He died in surgery.

Ralph had a hard time accepting his father's death. For years he believed his father would return one day.[1] The family was thrown into poverty. It was up to Ralph's

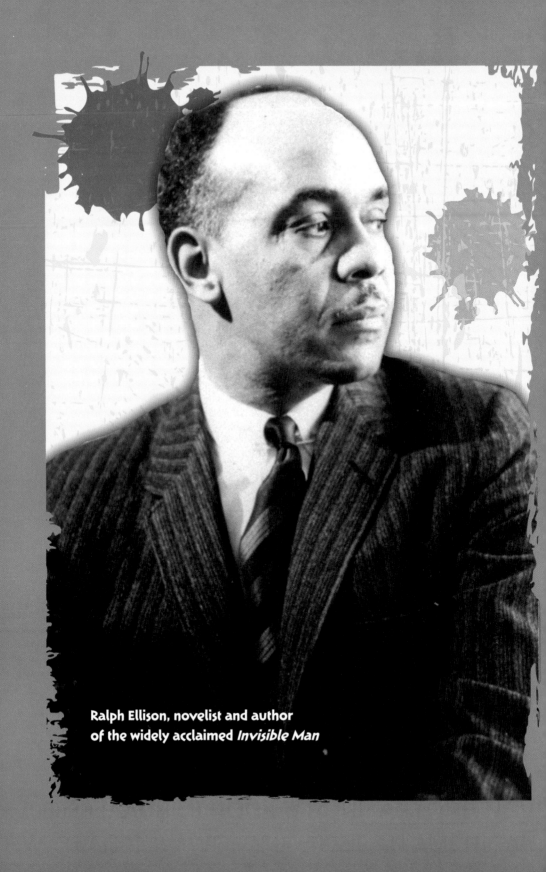

Ralph Ellison, novelist and author of the widely acclaimed *Invisible Man*

mother, Ida, to support him and his brother, Herbert. Not many jobs were available for African-American women. Ida took work as a nanny and a maid. She brought home discarded books and magazines from the wealthy homes where she worked for her children to read.

Music at Tuskegee

As a teenager, Ralph fell in love with jazz in the clubs of Oklahoma City. His school had an excellent music program. He learned to play trumpet and piano, and won a scholarship to study music at the Tuskegee Institute in Alabama. Not having enough money to buy a train ticket, he hopped aboard a freight train. It was 1933 and the country was in the midst of the Great Depression. Ralph had quite a fright when two armed railroad agents rounded up all of the illegal passengers.[2] He escaped, but it served as a wake-up call. If he got in trouble with the law in the Deep South, he would not be treated fairly because of the color of his skin.

Harlem Renaissance and a Turn to Writing

Ellison did not complete his degree at Tuskegee. There was a problem with his scholarship. He did not have enough money to pay for his final year. He left Alabama for New York City in the summer of 1936. He planned to make enough money as a musician to return to school. Ellison arrived in New York at the end of the Harlem Renaissance. It was a time of rich artistic expression in the African-American community. He soon met some highly creative artists, including Richard Wright. Wright encouraged Ellison to write fiction.[3]

41

Work as a musician was hard to find. From 1938 until 1942, Ellison worked as a researcher for the Federal Writers' Project (FWP). The FWP was part of President

Franklin D. Roosevelt's New Deal. The New Deal created jobs during the Depression. Ellison went on to edit a literary magazine, *The Negro Quarterly*. At the outbreak of World War II, he signed up for the Merchant Marines for two years. While on sick leave, he came up with the idea for his novel. After his stint in the service, Ellison returned to Harlem. There he met the great love of his life, Fanny McConnell. They were married in 1946. Fanny worked to support him during the seven years he took to write *Invisible Man*.

Invisible Man

The main character of the book is not really invisible, but he feels that way. No matter what he does, people refuse to see him. Instead they just see what they want to see. The story follows its unnamed character on his adventures through America. He leaves his home in the South to go to college on scholarship. Though he has done nothing wrong, he is soon expelled from school in disgrace. He travels to New York City in search of work. He gets a job in a paint factory, where he helps mix white paint. A fire breaks out and he is lucky to get out in time. For a while he acts as a spokesperson for a political group, only to find he is being used. He barely escapes an angry mob by diving through a hole in the sidewalk. He hides away in a basement to think over his plight. There, holed up underground, he decides to become a writer. He hopes that writing will help him make sense of his world, and make a name for himself on his own terms.

42

The book gained immediate praise from the literary world. Critics hailed it as a leap forward in writing about issues of race.[4] Ellison wrote about a person looking for his place in the world. It was a universal search. He wove diverse elements of American life into his book. He wrote about black folklore and Greek myth. He also referred to more modern authors, among them Irish novelist James Joyce, American writer Mark Twain, and Russian novelist Fyodor Dostoevsky. A 1965 *Book Week* poll named *Invisible Man* as the most distinguished post–World War II novel.

Invisible Man and the National Book Award

After Ellison won the National Book Award, he was in demand as a speaker. People saw him as a talented new voice in postwar American literature. He won a Rockefeller Foundation award in 1954 and lectured in Germany and Austria. In 1955 he won a fellowship from the American Academy of Arts and Letters and spent a year in Rome. In the late 1950s he took a job as a literature professor at Bard College. All the while he was at work on a sweeping second novel.

In 1964 Ellison released *Shadow and Act*, a collection of essays about American culture. He continued to teach classes, now at Rutgers and Yale. Although he still lectured, a younger generation of African Americans began to reject his work. As party to the militant Black Power movement, they wanted revolutionary heroes who took action, not literary ones who retreated underground.[5] During the 1970s, Ellison held the Albert Schweitzer Professor of Humanities chair at New York University. In 1975 he was elected to the American Academy of Arts and Letters. In 1985 he was awarded the National Medal of the Arts. In 1986 he released a second collection of essays, *Going to the Territory*.

43

Juneteenth

The Ellisons owned a house in the Berkshires of western Massachusetts. They would go there to escape the heat of the Harlem summer. In 1967, a fire broke out

On June 13, 1974, Ellison was awarded an honorary degree from Harvard University. The recipients are (back row from left): Jerome B. Wiesner, Ralph Ellison, Mstislav Rostropovich, Clifford Geertz, and Monsignor Rev. Helder Camara. Sitting in the front row from left are Beverly Sills, Harvard University President Derek Bok, and Chien Shiung Wu.

at their summer home. Ellison announced that the fire had destroyed his novel-in-progress. Arnold Rampersad, who wrote a recent biography of Ellison, is not so sure. He makes the case that the novel was not lost in the fire.[6] Though Ellison worked on it for many years, he never did complete a second novel. After his death, his widow turned thousands of pages of his writing over to his friend John Callahan. Callahan sifted through the unfinished work to create a novel. The result, *Juneteenth*, was published in 1999. The title refers to the day of June 19, 1865. That was when Texas slaves in Galveston first heard the news that slavery had been abolished two years earlier.[7]

A Statue in Harlem

Ralph Ellison died on April 16, 1994. A statue in his honor stands in Riverside Park in Harlem. The apartment where he and his wife lived for more than forty years is nearby. The memorial is a large bronze rectangle. In the center is the cutout figure of a man: an invisible man. Perhaps the best memorial to Ellison, however, is that his novel has never gone out of print.

Ralph Ellison Timeline

1914—Ralph Ellison is born on March 1 in Oklahoma City.

1917—Ellison's father, Lewis, dies.

1933—Ellison attends the Tuskegee Institute in Alabama to study music.

1936—Ellison is forced to leave Tuskegee after three years, and moves to Harlem.

1937—Ellison meets Richard Wright.

1938—Ellison gets a job with the Federal Writers' Project.

1946—Ellison marries Fanny McConnell.

1952—*Invisible Man* is published.

1954—Ellison wins Rockefeller Foundation award.

1964—*Shadow and Act*, a collection of essays, is published.

1970—Ellison becomes the Albert Schweitzer Professor of Humanities at New York University.

1985—Ellison is awarded the National Medal of Arts.

1986—*Going to the Territory*, a second collection of essays, is published.

1994—Ellison dies of cancer on April 16.

James Baldwin

James Baldwin is best known as the author of the novels *Go Tell It on the Mountain*, *Giovanni's Room*, and *Another Country*. He was also a civil rights activist, famous for his powerful essays on race and identity, especially as collected in *The Fire Next Time*.

Growing Up Poor in Harlem

James Arthur Jones was born in Harlem in 1924. His mother, Emma Berdis Jones, had moved to New York City from Maryland as a young woman. When James was three years old, his mother married David Baldwin. David worked six days a week in a factory, but still there was never enough money. He grew angry and bitter. He often took out his pent-up rage on his family. Emma worked as a maid. James was the eldest child. He often had the job of caring for his eight younger brothers and sisters. Even with both parents working, the family lived in extreme poverty. They had to move many times when they could not make rent.

On Sundays James's father would dress in his best clothes and preach at a nearby storefront church.

47

Author and activitist
James Baldwin

He spoke about the evil ways of the "white devils." David Baldwin tried to protect his children from the harsh world. He did not allow them to play outside in the street with other kids. When James was a teenager he learned the truth: This man was not his true father. This may have explained why his father often berated him, telling him he was ugly and frog-eyed.[1]

Though life at home was unbearable at times, James excelled at school. One teacher, Orilla Miller, visited his home. She came to ask permission to take James to a play. She was appalled at the family's poor living conditions.[2] James also studied under Countee Cullen, one of the great poets of the Harlem Renaissance. His teachers helped him see that there was a larger world outside of his father's strict house.

Preaching the Gospel

When he was fourteen, James had a religious experience: He believed that God called on him to become a preacher. For three years he preached at the Fireside Pentecostal Assembly in Harlem. He had a way with language and was an inspirational speaker.[3] During the school week James lived in a different world. He studied alongside his friends, most of them white and Jewish, at the prestigious all-boys DeWitt Clinton High School in the Bronx. He edited *The Magpie*, the school magazine, and contributed many of his own short stories. In his senior year he broke from the church and turned to writing. Next to his photograph in the school yearbook, Baldwin stated his ambition: to be a famous novelist and playwright.

49

Loss, Rioting, and Despair

The summer of 1943 was a troubled one for Harlem. The heat had been unbearable, and everyone was on

edge. When the news broke that a white police officer had shot a black soldier, people in Harlem rioted in the streets. They threw bricks at store windows and looted. Before the night was through, five people were dead, and more than five hundred injured.[4] During the riots, James's stepfather died in a mental hospital. On the day of his death, his wife gave birth to their daughter, Paula. The funeral procession wound through streets filled with broken glass. James knew he could not live there any longer.[5] He had to get out. He had wanted to attend college, but he could not. His family needed him as a wage earner.

Baldwin and a friend moved to Belle Meade, New Jersey, to take a well-paying job in the white-dominated construction industry. But there he encountered racism as he never had in all-black Harlem. It was unbearable. At age nineteen Baldwin moved back to New York City, this time to the artsy neighborhood of Greenwich Village, where he waited tables. He began to publish reviews and essays in magazines. A friend introduced him to his idol, Richard Wright. The older writer was impressed and secured a grant so that Baldwin could focus on the novel he was writing. It was a story about the awakening of a young man, a storefront preacher much like himself. No matter how he tried, he could not get the story quite right. Life in New York was getting him down. He was exhausted from working several jobs to help support his family. Something needed to change.

Escape to Paris

In 1948 Baldwin was awarded a Rosenwald Grant and scraped together enough money for a one-way ticket to Paris. Paris was renowned as a city of writers and intellectuals. It was also rumored to be a place where race issues were not so difficult.[6] Baldwin found the freedom there to concentrate on his writing. He published an essay titled "Everybody's Protest Novel" which criticized, among other things, Richard Wright's work. The two men had been friendly, but now their relationship was strained.

In the winter of 1951, Baldwin went to stay with friends in a small Swiss village high in the Alps. There he was finally able to finish the novel he had been working on for ten years. *Go Tell It on the Mountain* came out in 1953 to positive reviews.[7] This was followed by a well-received book of essays entitled *Notes of a Native Son* in 1955. He had also completed a play, *The Amen Corner*, but his publisher was not interested in it.

Inspired by his successes, Baldwin set to work on his next novel, *Giovanni's Room*. It was the story of expatriates living in France. It discussed the then-taboo topics of interracial relationships and love between men. When it was complete, he sent the manuscript to his publisher, who turned it down. The publisher did not think the American public was ready for its subjects.[8] This was their loss: Another publisher scooped it up and published *Giovanni's Room* in 1956. The book sold well. Within six weeks it was in its second printing.[9] Later that year Baldwin won an award from the National Institute of Arts and Letters.

The American Civil Rights Movement

51

In France, Baldwin was living comfortably as a writer. He enjoyed traveling and split his time between Paris, southern France, and Istanbul, Turkey. But in 1957 he decided it was time to return home. Times were changing in America. The U.S. Supreme Court's 1954 holding in *Brown v. Board of Education of Topeka, Kansas* that racial segregation in public education was unconstitutional energized the nation. African Americans, under the leadership of Rev. Martin Luther King Jr., sought to desegregate the South through peaceful demonstrations. They protested on buses and in schools. There was a backlash from white supremacists, who resisted these changes. The Ku Klux Klan burned crosses to create fear.

During the March on Washington on August 28, 1963, James Baldwin is shown shaking hands with actor Marlon Brando. Actor Charlton Heston and singer Harry Belafonte are behind Baldwin.

Federal troops were deployed to support desegregation at Little Rock's Central High School. It was a frightening and important time in American history, and Baldwin wanted to be a part of it. He visited the American South, where he met Dr. King and took part in protests. In 1961 he published a collection of essays about race in the United States titled *Nobody Knows My Name: More Notes of a Native Son*. It was a timely book and received great reviews. But by speaking out for change, Baldwin attracted the attention of the Federal Bureau of Investigation. The FBI began an extensive file on him.

Baldwin's third novel, *Another Country*, also came out in 1962. It told the story of a jazz musician's last days before committing suicide. It explored the unbearable toll of racism on a person. The book hit the bestseller charts. The following year, he released another book of essays, *The Fire Next Time*. The essays reflect his thoughts on race in America. During this time he was traveling throughout the South, lecturing and writing. He appeared on the cover of *Time* magazine. Baldwin was becoming a spokesperson for the civil rights movement as well as an important American writer. In 1964 he was elected to the National Institute of Arts and Letters.

Under Fire

Baldwin's fourth novel, *Tell Me How Long the Train's Been Gone*, came out in 1968. The story is about a black actor and his struggle to be true to himself. In his work, Baldwin often expressed that love and acceptance are the path to redemption. But in the late 1960s, this idea came under fire. Black militant groups preached that a violent uprising was needed to overthrow white society. They saw Baldwin as a pawn of white society.[10] On April 4, 1968, Rev. Martin Luther King Jr. was assassinated.

53

Baldwin went to Atlanta for his friend's funeral. He felt angry. Were the militants right? Was violence the only way real change could come about? He struggled to come to terms with his friend's death.

Baldwin's next novel, *If Beale Street Could Talk*, came out in 1974. In this love story set in Harlem, he explored the importance of family and love in the midst of crisis. In 1978 Baldwin taught his first of several classes in literature at Bowling Green State University in Ohio. His final novel, *Just Above My Head*, came out in 1979. This was followed by a book of poetry, *Jimmy's Blues: Selected Poems*, in 1983. In the mid–1980s he taught Afro-American Studies at the University of Massachusetts at Amherst.

The Legacy of an American Hero

Baldwin's writings earned him many national awards, among them the Certificate of Recognition of the National Institute of Arts and Letters (1956), the George Polk Award (1963), the Partisan Review Fellowship (1956), membership in the National Institute of Arts and Letters (1964), and induction to the Legion of Honor by the government of France (1986).

Baldwin returned to his home in the south of France in 1987. He was at work on a play called *The Welcome Table*, and he was also resting. A test earlier in the year had revealed cancer in his esophagus. He passed away at home on December 1. His body was buried in Hartsdale, New York. Baldwin's work continues to be held in high esteem. He had a powerful way with language, and was brave in speaking out against social injustices.

James Baldwin Timeline

1924—James Baldwin is born on August 2 in Harlem.

1938–1940—Baldwin is a youth minister at his stepfather's church.

1948—Baldwin moves to Paris, France.

1953—*Go Tell It on the Mountain* is published.

1954—Baldwin receives a Guggenheim Fellowship.

1955—*Notes of a Native Son* is published.

1956—*Giovanni's Room* is published.

1961—*Nobody Knows My Name: More Notes of a Native Son*, a collection of essays, is published.

1962—*Another Country* is published.

1963—*The Fire Next Time* is published.

1965—Baldwin's play *Blues for Mister Charlie* is performed on Broadway.

1965—Another of Baldwin's plays, *The Amen Corner*, is performed on Broadway.

1968—*Tell Me How Long the Train's Been Gone* is published.

1974—*If Beale Street Could Talk* is published.

1979—*Just Above My Head* is published.

1983— *Jimmy's Blues: Selected Poems* is published.

1985—*The Evidence of Things Not Seen* is published.

1987—Baldwin dies on December 1, at his home in St. Paul de Vence, France.

Chapter 6

Alex Haley

When Alex Haley's book hit the shelves in 1976, it became an international bestseller. *Roots: The Saga of an American Family* catapulted him to fame. *Roots* was made into a television miniseries. One hundred and thirty million people watched. It broke the record for largest television audience. Haley's book sparked a national interest in genealogy.

Boyhood in Henning

Alexander Murray Palmer Haley was born on August 11, 1921, in Ithaca, New York. His father, Simon Haley, was a graduate student at Cornell University. Simon and his wife, Bertha Palmer Haley, had met at college back home in Tennessee. Bertha was the only child of a well-to-do business owner. She worked as a music teacher. When Alex was born, the excited young parents returned to Henning, Tennessee, to show off their baby to his grandparents. Then Simon returned to Cornell to finish his degree. Bertha and the baby stayed behind to be with family. Alex Haley spent the first eight years of his life in Henning.[1]

American author Alex Haley's *Roots* won the National Book Award and received a special Pulitzer Prize.

Alex's mother taught school during the day, so he stayed with his maternal grandmother, Cynthia Palmer. She would sit in her rocking chair on her front porch and tell stories. One story was about her "furthest back ancestor," a man she called the African. His name was Kunta Kinte. When he was a young man, Kunta Kinte had taken a walk in the forest. He was looking for wood to make a drum when four men attacked him. They put him in shackles and took him forcibly onto a ship with many other kidnapped people. Conditions on the ship were horrible. The slave runners packed people onto shelves. They were chained together at the wrists and ankles.

When the ship landed in Annapolis, Maryland, two and a half months later, Kunta Kinte was sold into slavery.[2] He often thought of his family, far away, and wondered how they were. He tried to run away many times, until some slave catchers cut off his foot to punish him. When he had his own daughter, Kizzy, he told her this story. Kizzy told her children, and her children told their children. Now it was Alex's grandmother's turn to tell him. Alex's mother was not interested in the stories. She considered them "old-timey." She told her mother to stop talking about the past. She was looking toward the future, away from slavery and toward better days. Young Alex did not agree. He loved his grandmother's stories.[3]

After earning his degree, Alex's father returned to Henning. He and Bertha had two more sons, George and Julius. The family left Henning when he accepted a job at a college in Alabama. Alex often returned and spent many summers with his grandmother. When he was ten years old, his mother died after a long illness. Two years later, his father remarried a fellow professor at the college. The family soon grew to include a new baby sister, Lois.

Coast Guard Days

When Alex graduated from high school, he was unsure what he wanted to do for work. He attended college for two years. He entered the Coast Guard as a mess boy in 1939. His ship carried cargo and ammunition—a dangerous combination—to the Southwest Pacific during World War II. They were away at sea for months at a time. He filled his spare time by reading and writing letters home. He read every book on board. He started a side business writing letters for his fellow seamen to send to their girlfriends. He wrote adventure stories, hoping to have one published in a magazine.[4] He mailed off many stories and received many rejection slips. Finally, *eight years later*, a magazine accepted one of his stories. After transferring to the New York Coast Guard Personnel Separation Center, he was promoted to Editor of the Coast Guard publication *The Helmsman*, and assigned the title of Journalist, First Class.

Following His Dreams: A New Career

After twenty years with the Coast Guard, Haley held the post of Chief Journalist. In fact, he was the first member of the Coast Guard to hold the job of Journalist.[5] Though only thirty-seven, he was eligible to retire. Having been published by men's adventure magazines, he sought to write full-time. In 1959 he moved to Greenwich Village in New York City, home to many writers and artists. For a while he struggled to earn enough to get by. He was down to eighteen cents and two cans of sardines when he got his first check in the mail from a magazine. It provided enough encouragement for Haley to stick with his dreams.[6]

Haley's perseverance once again paid off. He soon began to get regular assignments from *Reader's Digest*

and the *Saturday Evening Post*. This led to a breakthrough. In 1962 he interviewed jazz great Miles Davis for *Playboy* magazine. It was a hard-hitting interview. Though the two men discussed jazz music, they also talked openly about race issues. The interview was controversial. It got people talking; just what the editors had hoped for.[7] The *Playboy* Interview became a regular feature. Haley went on to interview many famous people for the magazine. He talked with heavyweight champion boxer Cassius Clay, who changed his name to Muhammad Ali when he became a Muslim. He interviewed the great civil rights leader Rev. Martin Luther King Jr. before King's assassination. In fact, three of the men Haley interviewed were assassinated. This demonstrates how controversial his subjects often were.

The Autobiography of Malcolm X

One of Haley's famous interviews was with a Black Muslim leader named Malcolm X. The Black Muslims believed that American society could only be rid of white racism through a violent uprising. A publisher approached Haley with an idea. Would he conduct more interviews with Malcolm X and write a book? Over the course of two years, the two men collaborated to write *The Autobiography of Malcolm X*. As a teenager, Malcolm Little had turned to a life of street crime. After spending years in jail, he cleaned up his act and converted to the Black Muslim sect of Islam. After leaving jail he changed his name to Malcolm X and became a leader of the movement. A charismatic speaker, he quickly gained a following. But the Black Muslims felt he was growing too powerful.[8] In time, Malcolm X rejected their teachings that white people were the devil. Instead he preached the message of Islam that all men are brothers. He was

61

Alex Haley in U.S. Coast Guard uniform

assassinated in 1965, just weeks before the manuscript of the book was complete. When the book came out later that year, it sold millions of copies.

The success of *The Autobiography of Malcolm X* owes to the mystique of the Nation of Islam (NOI) and the audacity of Malcolm X. Americans didn't know what to make of the NOI, a proud, black, highly disciplined militant separatist group. Malcolm X had become the voice of the NOI, saying out loud to white America things that many African Americans only whispered among themselves. Millions bought Haley's book-length interview with Malcolm X to understand this unfiltered black anger.

Solving the Mystery of the Past: *Roots*

Haley began to think about the story of Kunta Kinte. From his grandmother's stories, he remembered that Kunta Kinte had called a guitar a *ko*. And he had called the river *Kamby Bolongo*. Could he use these words to solve the mystery of where Kinte had come from? He found a professor who specialized in African languages. To his amazement, Haley learned from him that Kinte had spoken Mandinka. The Mandingo people of Gambia speak this language. Haley traveled to Africa to the village of Juffure in Gambia. There he met with a tribal elder called a griot. (Griots are oral historians who commit the history of their tribe to memory.) The griot confirmed that a young man named Kunta Kinte had disappeared many generations ago. Haley spent years researching his book to get the facts right. He considered *Roots* "faction": a blend of fact and fiction.[9] It was based on a true story. Haley added emotion, dialogue, and descriptions to make it feel real.

With *Roots*, Haley hoped to restore a sense of identity and pride to African Americans.[10] Everywhere he went he was thanked for writing the book. *Roots* helped people begin the healing process over the terrible crime of slavery. Haley became a public speaker in high demand. He won the 1976 National Book Award for *Roots*. The following year he received the Pulitzer Prize. He was also awarded the Spingarn Medal from the NAACP.

Final Return to Henning

Despite his fame, Haley continued to make time to write. However, he never recreated the wild success of *Roots*. In

1988 he published *A Different Kind of Christmas*, a novella about a slave escape. He was at work on a book about his father's side of the family at the time of his death. It was published posthumously as *Queen. Mama Flora's Family*, another book based on Haley's writing, was published in 1998.

Haley died of a heart attack in 1992 while on a speaking tour in Seattle, Washington. He left an estate valued at $2 million. His remains were buried in Henning on the grounds of his grandmother's home where he first heard the story of Kunta Kinte. The house is now a historic site owned by the state of Tennessee.

Alex Haley Timeline

1921—Alex Haley is born on August 11, in Ithaca, New York.

1939—Haley joins the U.S. Coast Guard.

1941—Haley marries Nannie Branch.

1949—Haley receives the rank of first-class petty officer in the rate of journalist. He is promoted to chief journalist of the Coast Guard.

1954—Haley and Branch divorce. Haley marries Juliette Collins.

1959—Haley retires from the Coast Guard, and moves to Greenwich Village in New York City.

1962—Haley is hired to do an interview with Miles Davis for *Playboy* magazine.

1965— The *Autobiography of Malcolm X* is published.

1976—*Roots: The Saga of an American Family* is published, and Haley wins the National Book Award.

1977—*Roots* is turned into a miniseries on ABC. Haley is also awarded the Spingarn Medal from the NAACP, and the Pulitzer Prize.

1988—*A Different Kind of Christmas* is published.

1992—Haley dies on February 10, in Seattle, Washington, while on a lecture tour.

1993—*Queen* is published posthumously.

Toni Morrison

Toni Morrison is the author of nine novels and two works of nonfiction. She was the first African American to receive the Nobel Prize in Literature, in 1993. Her best-known novel is *Beloved*. It is a ghost story that takes place ten years after the Civil War. This powerful tale is about remembering the past in order to heal the wounds left by slavery. The book earned Morrison the Pulitzer Prize for Fiction in 1988.

A Childhood of Storytelling

Toni Morrison was born on February 18, 1931. Her family lived in Lorain, Ohio. Her parents gave her the name Chloe Anthony Wofford. In college, she grew fed up with people mispronouncing her name.[1] She changed it to Toni, short for her middle name. Her parents were George Wofford and Rahmah Willis Wofford. Their families had fled the South in the early part of the century. They wanted to escape the hardships of sharecropping and make a better life. Her father remained distrustful of white men throughout his life.[2] He found work as a

Award-winning novelist Toni Morrison

welder, and then in a factory. He often worked two or three jobs at a time to provide for his family.

Storytelling was a central part of Toni's childhood. The second child in the family, she had an older sister and two younger brothers. Though her father's parents had passed away by the time she was born, she grew up with her maternal grandparents. She had a close-knit family. To entertain the children, the adults told stories. Some were stories they had heard as children. Some were true stories about the past. Her father was particularly good at telling a tale. The children would huddle together to listen to his ghost stories.

An Academic

Toni did well in school. She loved to read. Her favorite authors were English novelist Jane Austen and Russian writers Leo Tolstoy and Fyodor Dostoevsky.[3] She graduated with honors from Lorain High School. Her mother took jobs as a domestic so that she could go on to college. She attended Howard University in Washington, D.C. There she studied English and the classics. Toni joined the drama club. When they toured the South, she saw first-hand the racism her parents had left behind. After earning her bachelor's degree, she went to Cornell University in Ithaca, New York. She graduated in 1955 with a master's degree in English. After teaching at Texas Southern University, she returned to Howard in 1957 to teach English.

Writing to Escape

While at Howard, she met a Jamaican architect, Howard Morrison. The couple married in 1958. They had two sons, Harold and Slade. But the marriage was not a happy one. Morrison found escape in a writing group.

Each week she was supposed to bring in something she had written to share with the others. One week she wrote a short story about a black girl who wished she had blue eyes. People told her it was a good story, and she filed it away.

In 1964 Morrison and her husband divorced. To earn money to support her young children, she took a job working for Random House. She moved to Syracuse, New York, to edit textbooks. She worked during the day while a housekeeper watched her sons. After work she would play with her boys. Once the children were in bed for the night, Morrison would sit down to write. She developed her story about the girl who longed for blue eyes into a novel, *The Bluest Eye*. It is a tragedy set in a small, black community in the 1940s. The main character, Pecola, is an abused girl who does not see her own beauty. She thinks people will love her only if she has blue eyes. After shopping the story around a bit, Morrison found a publisher who was interested.[4] *The Bluest Eye* was published in 1970.

Influential in the World of Publishing

In 1967 Morrison got a promotion at Random House. She moved to the company's headquarters in New York City. She rose through the ranks to become a senior editor. There were very few black senior editors in that field at the time. She had a great influence in bringing the works of many African-American authors to the public. She edited the books of Gayle Jones, Angela Davis, and Toni Cade Bambara. She worked with prizefighter Muhammad Ali when he wrote his autobiography. One of her most notable successes was *The Black Book*.[5] It was one of the first history books of its kind. It told the stories of everyday African Americans. It used primary source

Author Toni Morrison poses with a copy of her book *Beloved* in New York City in September 1987.

documents such as photographs and bills of sale from slave auctions.

In her spare time, Morrison continued to write. Her second book came out in 1973. *Sula* is the story of a friendship between two black women, Sula and Nel. The book was nominated for the National Book Award. People began to take notice of Morrison. She used language in a beautiful and poetic way. Her characters were strong and complex. She wrote with honesty and tackled difficult subjects. Morrison was invited to lecture at Yale University for the 1976–77 school year.

Her third book, *Song of Solomon*, was published in 1977. It tells the story of Milkman, a character who travels to the South to unravel a family mystery. The book was her most successful to date. It sold well, climbing onto the *New York Times* bestseller list. Critics praised it. She won her first major award: the National Book Critics Circle Award. *Song of Solomon* was a Book-of-the-Month Club selection. (The last time the club had featured a black author was in 1940 with Richard Wright's *Native Son*.) President Jimmy Carter nominated Morrison to the National Council on the Arts. The American Academy of Arts and Letters voted her the Distinguished Writer of the Year.

Morrison's next novel, *Tar Baby*, came out in 1981. It, too, was well received. The book's title referred to the folktales of Brer Rabbit. Morrison appeared on the cover of *Newsweek*. She was elected to the American Academy of Arts and Letters.

71

A Master of American Literature

In 1984 Morrison left her job at Random House. She took the Albert Schweitzer Professorship of Humanities at the State University of New York (SUNY) at Albany. While at SUNY, she wrote a play, *Dreaming Emmett*. She based it on the true story of Emmett Till, a fourteen-year-old boy lynched in 1955 for allegedly whistling at a white woman. The play was performed in 1986. It won the New York State Governor's Art Award.

When *Beloved* came out in 1987, Morrison's fame rose to new heights. The story is set in Ohio after the Civil War. It is the story of Sethe, a former slave who is haunted by a ghost. With the help of family, love, and community, she is able to exorcise the ghost. When they examine the past, the characters are able to begin to heal. The book immediately made the *New York Times* bestseller list. The following year it won the Pulitzer Prize. In 1998 a film version of *Beloved*, starring Danny Glover and Oprah Winfrey and directed by Jonathan Demme, was released. In May 2006 the *New York Times Book Review* called *Beloved* the best American novel of the last twenty-five years.

Since 1989 Morrison has held a chair at Princeton University. She is the Robert F. Goheen Professor of Humanities. She is the first black woman to hold a named chair at an Ivy League college. Her writing pace has not faltered. Her novel *Jazz* came out in 1992. It takes place in Harlem during the 1920s. Like jazz music, the book weaves together many voices to tell a story. Her novel *Paradise* (1998) tells the story of a group of outcast women. They live on the outskirts of an all-black town of Ruby, Oklahoma. As in *Beloved*, spirits and humans live side by side.

Her novel *Love* came out in 2003. It tells the story of a wealthy resort owner, Bill Cosey. He has died, and two women mourn him. They fight over who should inherit his estate. Morrison's most recent book is *A Mercy* (2009). It takes place in the American colonies. Set in the

American writer Toni Morrison receives the Nobel Prize in Literature from King Carl XVI Gustaf of Sweden in Stockholm, Sweden, December 10, 1993. Morrison is the first black woman to receive this prize.

early days of the slave trade, the story combines many different voices. There is Jacob, a reluctant slave owner, and Florens, the young slave girl he accepts as payment for a debt. Florens struggles to understand why her mother gave her up. As in *Beloved*, Morrison explores themes of motherhood, love, and slavery.

Nobel Laureate

On becoming the first African American to win the Nobel Prize in Literature, Morrison gave thanks to God that her mother was still alive. She was happy to share the joy of the historic moment. Morrison uses stories to explore the human experience. She writes of life's terrible pain and of its great beauty.

Toni Morrison Timeline

1931—Toni Morrison, real name Chloe Anthony Wofford, is born on February 18.

1949—Morrison graduates from Lorain High School with honors.

1953—Morrison graduates from Howard University.

1955—Morrison receives her master's degree from Cornell University.

1958—Morrison marries Harold Morrison.

1961—Morrison's son, Harold, is born.

1964—Morrison's son, Slade, is born; she and Harold divorce.

1970— *The Bluest Eye* is published.

1973—*Sula* is published and nominated for the American Book Award, but does not win.

1977—*Song of Solomon* is published. It is the first Book-of-the-Month selection by an African-American author since *Native Son* by Richard Wright in 1940.

1981—*Tar Baby* is published.

1987—*Beloved* is published.

1988—*Beloved* wins the Pulitzer Prize for Fiction.

1989—Morrison joins the faculty of Princeton University. She is the Robert F. Goheen Professor of Humanities.

1993—Morrison wins the Nobel Prize in Literature, and her book *Jazz* is published.

1998—*Paradise* is published.

1998—*Beloved* is made into a movie starring Danny Glover and Oprah Winfrey

2002—Two children's books, *The Big Box* and *The Book of Mean People*, are published.

2003—*Love* and another children's book, *The Ant or the Grasshopper?*, are published.

2006—Morrison retires from Princeton University.

2009—*A Mercy* is published.

Ernest Gaines

Ernest Gaines is the author of six novels and two collections of short stories. One of his best-known novels, *A Lesson Before Dying*, won the National Book Critics Circle Award in 1993. Gaines writes about what he knows best: small-town life in his home state of Louisiana.

Fifth Generation in the Parish

Ernest J. Gaines was born to Manuel and Adrienne Gaines on January 15, 1933, in the small town of Pointe Coupe Parish, Louisiana. He was the eldest of seven children. They lived in the old slave quarters of the plantation where his family had lived for five generations. When Gaines was still a child, his father left the family. His mother went to New Orleans to find work. Ernest and his siblings stayed behind in Pointe Coupe with family. They were raised by their great aunt, Miss Augusteen Jefferson. Miss Jefferson was a hard-working woman. Her legs were crippled. Because she could not walk, she pulled herself along the floor with her arms. She sat on

Ernest Gaines writes about the rural South, where he grew up.

a bench by the woodstove to cook. She pulled herself down the porch steps to sit in the garden, pulling weeds. Gaines credits his aunt as the greatest influence of his life.[1] He remembers her handling her disability "with true dignity."[2]

Family and friends came to her house to visit. In the summer evenings, people gathered on the gallery, or front porch, to talk. They kept their hands busy, shelling peas or piecing together quilt squares. They had no radios or televisions. Talking and storytelling was their entertainment. They spoke in English, switching to Creole when they did not want the children to understand what they said. Creole is a language spoken by the descendants of the French people who settled in Louisiana.

At the age of eight, Ernest began to work in the fields. He picked cotton for fifty cents a day. He learned his lessons in a one-room schoolhouse. Later he attended a Catholic school in the nearby town of New Roads. The plantation owner, a sheriff whom Gaines recalls as a decent man, gave him a ride to school each day.[3] The older people on the plantation had never learned to read and write. They relied on Ernest to read the paper aloud to them. They asked him to write letters for them to send to family who had moved away. They were not always sure what to say. Ernest grew good at writing down what he thought they might like to say, and doing it quickly. He wanted to get back to playing with his friends.[4]

Homesick

Though Ernest loved his home and his aunt, he moved away at age fifteen.[5] His mother had made up her mind: Ernest would be the first in the family to complete his schooling. There was no high school near Pointe Coupe.

79

So he boarded a bus and went west to California to live with his mother and stepfather. His stepfather worked in the Merchant Marines. They lived in the seaside town of Vallejo. His stepfather warned him not to hang out with the other boys in the neighborhood. They were a rough bunch, and he did not want Ernest to fall in with the wrong crowd. Homesick and with no friends, Ernest took solace in reading. He got a library card and took out all the books he could find about the South. At that time, the only southern books in the Vallejo Public Library were written by whites. Ernest found things that he liked in these books. He thought sometimes the writers did a good job capturing the sounds, sights, and smells of the countryside. However, he did not find the southern people he knew. He saw that he would have to be the one to write the book he was searching for.[6]

A Book Wrapped Up in String

When Gaines was sixteen, he wrote his first book. He wrote it out in longhand on lined yellow paper. When it was complete, his mother rented a typewriter for him. He spent his summer babysitting his newborn brother and pounding away at the typewriter. He cut the paper in half to look like pages from a real book. When it was complete, he wrapped it in brown paper and tied it up with string. He mailed it to a publisher in New York, hoping to hear any day that he had written a great masterpiece. When the bundle came back with a rejection slip, Gaines felt dejected. He took the package out to the backyard and burned it in the incinerator. But he did not give up on the idea of being a writer.[7]

After graduating from high school, Gaines was drafted into the army for two years and stationed in Guam. In his off-duty hours, he wrote. He entered a short story

into a military writing contest. His story took second place on Guam and received honorable mention on a national level. Upon leaving the army, Gaines enrolled at San Francisco State University with money from the G.I. Bill. When he met with his college adviser, he said he wanted to be a writer. His adviser informed him that very few people made a living by writing, and almost none of them were African-American. The college did not even offer a creative writing major at the time. Did he have a second choice? Gaines stated that he did not. Writing was what he wanted to do.[8] He decided to major in English. He published several short stories in *Transfer*, the college literary journal.

Making Ends Meet

Gaines graduated in 1957 with a B.A. in English literature. That same year, he won the Wallace Stegner Award, which recognizes outstanding contributions to the cultural identity of the West. This allowed him to spend a year studying at Stanford University in the Creative Writing Department. There he met his long-time editor, Dorothea Oppenheimer. They worked together until her death in 1987. In a 1986 interview Gaines commented, "She would suggest things, and it was her opinion I appreciated more than anyone else's."[9]

Gaines gave himself ten years to make it as a writer.[10] He turned down a teaching job so that he could focus on his writing. He took jobs to earn some much-needed money. He worked at the post office. He set type at a print shop. He washed dishes. And then in 1964, seven years after college, he published his first novel, *Catherine Carmier*. It was another version of the same story he had sent to the publisher in New York at age sixteen. It was a love story between a black man and a Creole woman.

His second novel, *Of Love and Dust*, was published in 1967. It is the story of a black man who has shot another black man in self-defense. He is convicted of murder but does not go to prison. Instead, he must serve his time working in the fields for a white man. Gaines was inspired by real-life events in the 1940s. He won the National Endowment for the Arts study grant in 1967. A book of his short stories, *Bloodline*, followed in 1968.

Popular Success: *The Autobiography of Miss Jane Pittman*

In 1970 Gaines received a Rockefeller Grant. At this time he was at work on a third novel. It would tell the story of a 110-year-old woman. She had been born a slave and lived to take part in the civil rights movement. At first Gaines wrote her story from the perspective of many different people. He wrote many drafts. In the end, he decided to let the woman tell her own story. His book *The Autobiography of Miss Jane Pittman* came out in 1971. It became a bestseller and was nominated for the Pulitzer Prize. Many people did not realize the book was a novel. They thought Miss Pittman must be a real person. A representative from *Newsweek* asked Gaines to mail her a photograph of Miss Pittman. Gaines explained Miss Pittman did not exist outside his imagination. His story was a work of fiction.[11] The story was made into a film. Actress Cicely Tyson won an Emmy for her portrayal of the title character.

Gaines's next novel, *In My Father's House*, came out in 1978. It is a story about fathers and sons searching for each other. He followed this with *A Gathering of Old Men* in 1983. Even though Gaines was living in San Francisco, he wrote about rural Louisiana. When the University of Southwestern Louisiana offered him a professorship in

Actress Cicely Tyson is seen in the title role of the TV miniseries adaptation of *The Autobiography of Miss Jane Pittman.*

creative writing, Gaines jumped at the chance to return home.[12] Since 1983 he has been a permanent writer-in-residence at the university.

A Lesson Before Dying

In 1993 Gaines published his masterpiece. *A Lesson Before Dying* tells the story of a small-town schoolteacher who befriends a death row inmate. The book won the National Book Critics Circle Award. It was nominated for the Pulitzer Prize in 1993. Though Gaines had eschewed marriage and children to focus on his career, now he married. His wife is Dianne Saulney, a Miami attorney and a Louisiana native he met in 1988. The couple divides their time between Miami, Louisiana, and San Francisco.

A Respected Writer

Gaines has received much acclaim for his books. He has been awarded Guggenheim and MacArthur fellowships. In 1998 he was voted into the Academy of Arts and Letters. He received the National Humanities Medal in 2000. In 2004 Gaines was nominated for the Nobel Prize in Literature. His work has been translated into French, Spanish, German, and Chinese. He retired from teaching in 2004. He resides at his home in the country, on the same land where his family has lived for more than a hundred years. His most recent book, *Mozart and Leadbelly: Stories and Essays* was released in 2005.

Ernest Gaines Timeline

1933—Ernest Gaines is born on January 15 in Pointe Coupe Parish, Louisiana.

1948—Gaines moves to Vallejo, California, to be with his mother and stepfather.

1950—Gaines joins the U.S. Army.

1952—Gaines enrolls at San Francisco State University.

1957—Gaines graduates with a B.A. in English literature and wins the Wallace Stegner Award.

1964—*Catherine Carmier* is published.

1967—*Of Love and Dust* is published, and Gaines wins a National Endowment for the Arts study grant.

1968—*Bloodline* is published.

1970—Gaines receives a Rockefeller Grant.

1971—*The Autobiography of Miss Jane Pittman* is published. Gaines is appointed writer-in-residence at Denison University.

1974—*The Autobiography of Miss Jane Pittman* is made into a TV miniseries, and wins nine Emmy Awards.

1978—*In My Father's House* is published.

1983— *A Gathering of Old Men* is published.

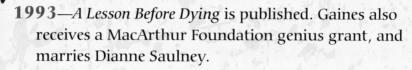

1993—*A Lesson Before Dying* is published. Gaines also receives a MacArthur Foundation genius grant, and marries Dianne Saulney.

2000— Gaines receives the National Humanities Medal.

2005—*Mozart and Leadbelly: Stories and Essays* is published.

Alice Walker

Alice Walker was twenty-six years old when she published her first novel in 1970. Critics were quick to call her a fresh new voice in American literature. Walker has gone on to become a world-renowned writer of novels and essays. In 1982 she became the first African-American woman to win the National Book Award, and also win the Pulitzer Prize for Fiction, for her third novel, *The Color Purple*. Walker is also an accomplished poet, with six volumes published to date.

Humble Beginnings

Alice Malsenior Walker was born on February 9, 1944, in rural Georgia. Her parents, Willie Lee and Minnie Tallulah Grant Walker, were sharecroppers in the town of Eatonton. Though they were poor, Alice's loving mother created a pleasant home for her family. She had a way with plants. People stopped in to admire her beautiful flower gardens.[1] Alice, the youngest of eight, was a bright and gifted child. When she was eight years old, she and her brothers were playing with BB guns. A pellet hit her

Alice Walker won the National Book Award and the Pulitzer Prize for her novel *The Color Purple.*

in the eye. Her father flagged down a car to take her to the hospital. The driver, a racist white man, refused to help and drove away. Walker lost sight in that eye. Milky scar tissue grew over her pupil. After the accident, she grew quiet and introverted, believing she was ugly.[2] She escaped inward into a world of reading and writing.

When Alice was fourteen, her older brother Bill invited her to visit him in Boston. He took Alice to an eye surgeon. She had surgery to remove the scar tissue. Though her vision did not return, her eye looked normal once again. When she returned home at the end of the summer, she had her confidence back.[3] She excelled in school once again and graduated at the top of her class. She made many friends and was even voted prom queen.

College Bound

In 1961 Walker left Eatonton on a Greyhound bus headed to Atlanta. She had a scholarship to attend Spelman College, an all-women's school in Atlanta, Georgia. Walker sat down in the front of the bus. A racist white woman complained that she did not belong there. The driver asked her to move to the back. As she walked to the back of the bus, Walker vowed to herself that she would help bring about change in the South.[4]

Her professors at Spelman saw Walker as a bright student with a talent for writing.[5] Her favorite, Dr. Howard Zinn, was a vocal supporter of the struggle for civil rights for African Americans. He encouraged students to take part in protesting Jim Crow laws. School officials did not agree and fired Zinn. Outraged, Walker wrote a letter of complaint to the school newspaper. She soon transferred to Sarah Lawrence College in Bronxville, New York. During her junior year, she traveled to Africa. Upon her return to the United States, she wrote poems

89

about Africa and her experiences growing up in the South. These were published in 1968 as *Once*. Walker graduated from Sarah Lawrence in January 1966 with a bachelor of arts degree. She thought about returning to Africa to study French.[6] Instead she booked a flight to Jackson, Mississippi. She would work to register African-American voters and to improve the lives of children. She would do her part to bring about change in the South.

Working for Change

It was in Jackson that Walker fell in love with a fellow civil rights worker. Mel Leventhal was a white, Jewish lawyer. He shared her passion for social justice. At the time it was illegal in the state of Mississippi for interracial couples to marry. They did not let that stop them: They married in New York City and returned to Jackson to live. Though they had many friends, it was still hard to be an interracial couple. Whenever they went out in public they were jeered at by whites and blacks alike.

Walker wrote and taught at Jackson State University and Tougaloo College. In 1969 she and Leventhal had a daughter, Rebecca. The following year her first novel came out. *The Third Life of Grange Copeland* told the story of three generations of an African-American family. Her book gained national acclaim. Walker wanted to write more, but she was growing weary of Mississippi. The strain was too much.[7] She was awarded a fellowship to the Radcliffe Institute in Cambridge, Massachusetts, in 1971. Walker took Rebecca north with her. There, free from the crushing day-to-day racism, she could focus on her writing. Leventhal remained behind to continue his civil rights work.

Finding Zora

Walker had read the works of many authors she admired. But most of them were men, and most were white. She found few writers she could truly identify with. While doing research for a story about voodoo, Walker stumbled across Zora Neale Hurston's book *Mules and Men*. At last she had found a role model. Here was a woman, an African-American woman, who had written about African-American culture. She had captured the language that Walker recognized from her own childhood in the South.[8]

Walker developed a black women writers class, which she taught at Wellesley College, an all-women's school outside of Boston. She used photocopies of Hurston's stories because her books were out of print; few people had even heard of Hurston. Walker's class is thought to be the first in the United States to focus on black women's literature.[9] After finishing her residency at Radcliffe in 1973, Walker traveled to Florida. She found the unmarked grave of Zora Neale Hurston. It was overgrown, and covered in weeds. Walker paid for a headstone. In 1979 she edited a Zora Neale Hurston reader. It was titled *I Love Myself When I Am Laughing...And Then Again When I Am Looking Mean and Impressive*. The book did much to bring Hurston's writing back into the mainstream.

Productive Years

Walker and her family moved to New York City. She continued to write. She also took a job as an editor for *Ms.* magazine. Her second novel, *Meridian*, came out in 1976. It took place during the civil rights movement. The book explored themes close to her heart: interracial marriage and motherhood. She won the National Institute of Arts and Letters Award. The same year she put out a

91

Alice Walker, left, and Robert Allen, editor of *Black Scholar*, look at a copy of Walker's *The Color Purple* at a screening of the film adaptation of the book in Eatonton, Georgia, in 1986.

biography for young people about the poet Langston Hughes. It was a busy time. In the midst of all this, she and her husband divorced.

In 1978 Walker received an award from the National Endowment for the Arts. She and her daughter moved to San Francisco. The Guggenheim Foundation granted her a fellowship. She bought some land out in the country where she could focus on a third novel. Little did she know that this story would soon catapult her into fame.

The Color Purple

When Walker's novel *The Color Purple* came out in 1982, it created quite a buzz. Today it is considered a masterpiece of American literature. It tells the story of a young black woman named Celie who overcomes physical and emotional abuse. It won both the American Book Award and the Pulitzer Prize for Fiction in 1983. Walker was the first African-American woman to win each of these prestigious awards. Her book remained on the *New York Times* bestseller list for twenty-five weeks in a row. Walker then released a book of essays, *In Search of Our Mothers' Gardens*, in 1983. The timing could not have been better. The book was well received by critics and the public alike. In it, she coined the term *womanism* to define her beliefs as a spiritual African-American woman. In 1985 Warner Bros. released a film version of *The Color Purple*. Steven Spielberg, of *Jaws* and *Indiana Jones* fame, directed it. The film starred Whoopi Goldberg, Danny Glover, and Oprah Winfrey.

93

A Life of Accomplishment

Walker had reached great success with *The Color Purple*. She did not rest on her laurels. Her writing has kept pace. Her fourth novel, *Temple of My Familiar*, came out in 1989.

It is an epic story about three couples that takes place over half a million years. In 1992 she released her fifth novel, *Possessing the Secret of Joy*. In this book, Walker shed light on female genital mutilation. This is a tribal custom practiced in parts of Africa and other parts of the world. She also worked on the documentary *Warrior Marks* (1994) with Indian-British filmmaker Pratibha Parmar on the same subject. Their work has helped curtail this brutal custom.

Walker's sixth novel, *By the Light of My Father's Smile*, came out in 1998. It is about an African-American missionary family. They learn from the Navajo people they have come to help. Her most recent novel, *Now Is the Time to Open Your Heart*, came out in 2004. It also explores spiritual themes and the healing power of nature. Her most recent work is a book of essays, *We Are the Ones We Have Been Waiting For.* It was released in 2006.

Alice Walker continues to speak up for what she believes to be right. She does so both as a writer and as an activist. She has publicly protested the United States' war in Iraq. In 2008 she traveled to Gaza in the Middle East with the antiwar group Code Pink. They protested Israeli use of force. Walker is admired for her bravery in searching for and speaking the truth.

Alice Walker Timeline

1944—Alice Walker is born on February 9 in Eatonton, Georgia.

1961—Walker attends Spelman College. She transfers to Sarah Lawrence College before her junior year.

1966—Walker graduates from Sarah Lawrence College with a bachelor of arts degree.

1967—Walker marries Mel Leventhal.

1968— *Once* is published.

1969—Walker's daughter, Rebecca, is born.

1970—*The Third Life of Grange Copeland* is published.

1971—Walker is awarded a fellowship to the Radcliffe Institute.

1976—*Meridian* is published. Walker and Leventhal divorce.

1979—Walker edits *I Love Myself When I Am Laughing… And Then Again When I Am Looking Mean and Impressive*, a collection of Zora Neale Hurston's works.

1982—*The Color Purple* is published.

1983—*The Color Purple* wins the American Book Award and the Pulitzer Prize for Fiction. *In Search of Our Mothers' Gardens*, a collection of essays, is published.

1985—*The Color Purple* is made into a movie.

1989— *Temple of My Familiar* is published.

1992— *Possessing the Secret of Joy* is published.

1998—*By the Light of My Father's Smile* is published.

2004—*Now Is the Time to Open Your Heart* is published.

2006—*We Are the Ones We Have Been Waiting For: Light in a Time of Darkness*, a collection of essays, and *There Is a Flower at the Tip of My Nose Smelling Me*, a picture book, are published.

Chapter Notes

Chapter 1
Harriet Adams Wilson

1. The Harriet Wilson Project, n.d., <http://www
   .harrietwilsonproject.org/about_harriet.htm> (May
   10, 2008).

2. Eric Gardner, "Of Bottles and Books: Reconsidering
   the Readers of Harriet Wilson's *Our Nig*," in *Harriet
   Wilson's New England: Race, Writing, and Region*, ed.
   JerriAnne Boggis, Eve Allegra Raimon, and Barbara
   A. White (Durham, N.H.: University of New
   Hampshire Press, 2007), p. 15.

3. The Harriet Beecher Stowe Center, "Harriet Beecher
   Stowe's Life," 2005, <http://www
   .harrietbeecherstowecenter.org/utc/> (January 9,
   2009).

4. Gardner, pp. 10–11.

5. The Harriet Wilson Project.

6. Eric Gardner, "Harriet E. Wilson. Our Nig; or,
   Sketches from the Life of a Free Black," *The Free
   Library*, December 22, 2004, <http://www
   .thefreelibrary.com/Harriet+E.+Wilson.+Our+Nig
   %3b+or%2c+Sketches+from+the+Life+of+a+
   Free... -a0132866637> (December 1, 2008).

7. Karen Marie Woods, "Harriet Adams Wilson", *Voices
   from the Gaps*, June 1, 1997 <http://voices
   .cla.umn.edu/vg/artistpages/WilsonHarriet.php>
   (November 21, 2008).

Chapter 2
Zora Neale Hurston

1. Valerie Boyd, "About Zora Neale Hurston," *The Official Zora Neale Hurston Website*, 2007, <www.zoranealehurston.com/biography.html> (November 10, 2008).

2. Zora Neale Hurston, *Dust Tracks on a Road: An Autobiography*, 2nd edition (Urbana: University of Illinois Press, 1984), p. 21.

3. Ibid., p. 32.

4. Ibid., pp. 45–46.

5. Boyd.

6. Hurston, p. 152.

7. Ibid. pp. 61–64.

8. Carla Kaplan, ed., *Zora Neale Hurston: A Life in Letters* (New York: Anchor Books, 2002), pp. 436–437.

9. Robert E. Hemenway, *Zora Neale Hurston: A Literary Biography* (Urbana: University of Illinois Press, 1980), p. 307.

10. Alice Walker, *Anything We Love Can Be Saved: A Writer's Activism* (New York: Ballantine Books, 1997), p. 46.

Chapter 3
Richard Wright

1. Richard Wright, *Later Works: Black Boy (American Hunger)* (New York: Library of America, 1991), pp. 15–16.

2. Ibid., p. 30.

3. Ibid., p. 49.

4. Ibid., p. 53

5. Ibid., pp. 46–47.

6. Ibid., pp. 159–161.

7. Ibid., p. 175.

8. Ibid., p. 237.

9. Ibid., p. 250.

10. Hazel Rowley, *Richard Wright* (New York: Henry Holt and Company, 2001), p. 254.

11. Federal Bureau of Investigation, "Richard Nathaniel Wright," *FBI Records: The Vault*, <http://vault.fbi.gov/Richard Nathaniel Wright> (February 8, 2009).

12. Rowley, pp. 231–232, 258.

13. Ibid., p. 326.

14. Saunders Redding, "The Long Dream," *The New York Times Book Review* (October 26, 1958), in *Richard Wright: Critical Perspectives Past and Present*, by Henry Louis Gates, Jr., and K. A. Appiah (New York: Amistad Press, 1993), pp. 60–61.

15. Rowley, p. 505.

Chapter 4
Ralph Ellison

1. John F Callahan, "Frequencies of Memory: A Eulogy for Ralph Waldo Ellison," in *The Critical Response to Ralph Ellison*, ed. Robert J. Butler (Westport, Conn.: Greenwood Press, 2000), pp. 202–203.

2. Ralph Ellison, *Going to the Territory* (New York: Random House, 1986), pp. 324–325.

3. Ibid., p. 203.

4. Butler, pp. xx–xxi.

5. Robert B. Stepto and Michael S. Harper, "Study and Experience: An Interview with Ralph Ellison," in Butler, p. 8.

6. Kevin Eagan, "Book Review: Ralph Ellison – A Biography by Arnold Rampersad," *BlogCritics Magazine*, February 21, 2008, <http://blogcritics .org/archives/2008/02/21/144546.php> (December 14, 2008).

7. Elizabeth Farnswoth, "Ralph Ellison's Legacy," PBS Online NewsHour, June 21, 1999, <http://www .pbs.org/newshour/bb/entertainment/jan-june99/ ellison_6-21.html> (December 5, 2008).

Chapter 5
James Baldwin

1. Michael Fabre, "Fathers and Sons in Baldwin's *Go Tell It on the Mountain*," in *James Baldwin: A Collection of Critical Essays*, ed. Keneth Kinnamon (Englewood Cliffs, N.J.: Prentice-Hall Inc., 1974), pp.133–134.

2. David Leeming, *James Baldwin: A Biography* (New York: Henry Holt and Company, 1995), p. 16.

3. James Campbell, *Talking at the Gates: A Life of James Baldwin* (New York: Viking Penguin, 1991), p. 10.

4. Jay Maeder, "Swelter Disturbance in Harlem, August 1943 Chapter 164," *New York Daily News*, August 14, 2000, <http://www.nydailynews.com/ archives/news/2000/08/14/2000-08-14_swelter_ disturbance_in_harle.html> (February 15, 2009).

5. Leeming, pp. 42–43.

6. Campbell, p. 52.

7. Leeming, p. 89.

8. Campbell, p. 96.

9. James Baldwin, *Early Novels and Stories*, ed. Toni Morrison (New York: Library of America, 1998), p. 957.

10. Ibid., p. 960.

Chapter 6
Alex Haley

1. Tennessee Historical Commission, State Owned Historic Sites, "Alex Haley House and Museum," February 7, 2005, <http://www.tn.gov/environment/hist/stateown/alexhaley.shtml> (February 16, 2009).

2. Alex Haley, *Alex Haley: The Playboy Interviews*, ed. Murray Fisher (New York: Ballantine Books, 1993), pp. 414–415.

3. Haley, p. 396.

4. Alex Haley, *Roots* (Garden City, N.Y.: Doubleday, 1976), p. 668.

5. Kunta Kinte–Alex Haley Foundation, Inc., *Roots*, "Alex Haley Biography," n.d., <http://www.kintehaley.org/rootshaleybio.html> (February 16, 2009).

6. Haley, *Alex Haley: The Playboy Interviews*, p. 397.

7. Haley, *Alex Haley: The Playboy Interviews*, pp. viii–ix.

8. Alex Haley, *The Autobiography of Malcolm X* (New York: Ballantine Books, 1965), p. 317.

9. Haley, *Roots*, p. 686.

10. Haley, *Alex Haley: The Playboy Interviews*, p. 432.

Chapter 7
Toni Morrison

1. Nellie L. McKay, introduction to *Toni Morrison's Beloved*, eds. William L. Andrews and Nellie Y. McKay (New York: Oxford University Press, 1999), p. 4.

2. Danille Taylor-Guthrie, ed., *Conversations with Toni Morrison* (Jackson, Miss.: University Press of Mississippi, 1994), p. 283.

3. University of Minnesota, *Voices from the Gaps*, "Artist Biography: Toni Morrison," February 2007, <http://voices.cla.umn.edu/artistpages/morrison_toni.html> (May 8, 2009).

4. McKay, p. 5.

5. Henry Louis Gates, Jr., and Cornel West, eds., *The African American Century* (New York: Simon & Schuster, 2000), p. 367.

Chapter 8
Ernest Gaines

1. John Lowe, "An Interview with Ernest Gaines/1994," in *Conversations with Ernest Gaines*, ed. John Lowe (Jackson: University Press of Mississippi, 1995), p. 322.

2. Ernest J. Gaines, *Mozart and Leadbelly: Stories and Essays* (New York: Alfred A. Knopf, 2005), p. 4.

3. Lowe, pp. 326–327.

4. Gaines, p. 30.

5. Ibid., pp. 5–6.

6. Gregory Fitzgerald and Peter Marchant, "An Interview: Ernest J. Gaines/1969," in *Conversations with Ernest Gaines*, p. 8.

7. Gaines, pp. 11–12.

8. Ibid., pp. 12–13.

9. Marcia Gaudet and Carl Wooton, "An Interview with Ernest J. Gaines/1986," in *Conversations with Ernest Gaines*, p. 213.

10. Jeannie Blake, "Interview with Ernest J. Gaines/1982," in *Conversations with Ernest Gaines*, p. 142.

11. Gaines, p. 3.

12. Ruth Laney, "Southern Sage Savors his Rise to Success," in *Conversation with Ernest Gaines*, p. 295.

Chapter 9
Alice Walker

1. Alice Walker, "In Search of Our Mothers' Gardens," *In Search of Our Mothers' Gardens* (San Diego: Harcourt Brace Jovanovich, 1983), p. 241.

2. Evelyn C. White, *Alice Walker: A Life* (New York: W.W. Norton and Co., 2004), p. 40.

3. Walker, "Beauty: When the Other Dancer Is the Self," *In Search of Our Mothers' Gardens*, pp. 366–367.

4. Walker, "Choosing to Stay at Home," *In Search of Our Mothers' Gardens*, p. 163.

5. White, p. 69.

6. Ibid., p. 130.

7. Ibid., pp. 206–207.

8. Walker, "Saving the Life That Is Your Own," *In Search of Our Mothers' Gardens*, pp. 9–12.

9. White, p. 222.

Glossary

abolition—the movement to end slavery in the United States

anthropology—the scientific study of human beings' culture, history, language, religions, and traditions

autobiography—a written account of the author's own life

blues—a type of music with roots in African-American culture of the rural South

charismatic—charming

circuit—a lecture tour

Civil War (U.S.)—a war fought between the northern and the southern states from 1861 through 1865 over the issues of states' rights and slavery

Communism—a political system in which all goods are shared equally by everyone

Creole—descendant of French settlers of Louisiana; also, the language they speak

dialect—a way of speaking that is particular to people from a certain area

Emancipation Proclamation—a declaration made by President Abraham Lincoln that outlawed slavery in areas in rebellion against the United States as of January 1, 1863

fellowship—a grant of money to support the work of an artist

fiction—a story that comes from the imagination of the author

folklore—the traditional stories and customs of a people

gallery—a Creole word for front porch

genealogy—the study of a person's family history

griot—an African tribal elder and storyteller who recounts from memory the history of the tribe

Harlem Renaissance—a creative period during the 1920s of African-American arts based in the New York neighborhood of Harlem

indentured servant—a person forced to work, often for many years or even a lifetime, to pay off a debt

jazz—a type of music that began in the United States in the early 1900s with roots in African-American blues music

Jim Crow laws— laws enacted by individual states after the Civil War that treated African Americans as second-class citizens

literary—having to do with written works, usually of fiction

medium—a person who claims to be in contact with the spirit world

novel—a lengthy story that comes from the imagination of its author

peddler—a traveling salesperson

protest—to speak out against something believed to be wrong

racism—judging people by the color of their skin

segregate—to separate people by race or ethnicity; to ban those groups from using public facilities such as schools, restrooms, water fountains, and restaurants

sharecropper—a farmer who rents farmland and receives a share of the crop

slave—a person whose rights are not recognized by society and who is treated as the property of a master

Spiritualism—a religious movement, popular in the 1800s, in which mediums claimed to communicate with the spirit world

Further Reading

Boggis, JerriAnne, Eve Allegra Raimon, and Barbara A. White, eds. *Harriet Wilson's New England: Race, Writing, and Region*. Durham: University of New Hampshire Press, 2007.

Ellison, Ralph. *The Collected Essays of Ralph Ellison*. New York: Modern Library, 2003.

Gaines, Ernest J. *Mozart and Leadbelly: Stories and Essays*. New York: Alfred A. Knopf, 2005.

Haley, Alex. *Alex Haley: The Man Who Traced America's Roots*. Pleasantville, N.Y.: Reader's Digest Association, 2007.

Hurston, Lucy Anne and the estate of Zora Neale Hurston. *Speak, So You Can Speak Again: The Life of Zora Neale Hurston*. New York: Doubleday, 2004.

Standley, Fred L. and Louis H. Pratt, eds. *Conversations with James Baldwin*. Jackson: University Press of Mississippi, 1989.

Taylor-Guthrie, Danille, ed. *Conversations with Toni Morrison*. Jackson: University of Mississippi, 1994.

Walker, Alice. *In Search Of Our Mothers' Gardens*. New York: Harcourt Brace Jovanovich, 1983.

Wright, Richard. *Black Boy (American Hunger: A Record of Childhood and Youth)*. New York: Harper Perennial, 2007.

Internet Addresses

African American Literature Book Club
<http://aalbc.com/>

Black Artists
<http://www.biography.com/blackhistory/
    people/artists.jsp>

Encyclopedia of World Biography
<http://www.notablebiographies.com/>

Index